mending broken

"In *Mending Broken* Teresa B Pasquale goes where only the bravest writers go: to the deepest and most true layer of experience. She takes this journey with honesty, insight and grace. You will learn things about yourself in these pages, which is what I always hope for in a book."

—Michele Rosenthal, author of *Before the World Intruded* + founder of www.healmyptsd.com

" This book is so helpful as it speaks from the heart. Reading this you'll emerge knowing you can be whole and fully alive, no matter what has happened in the past. We are blessed when people like Teresa B Pasquale, offers us the intimacy of their story, courage and healing - it shines light on the path of our journey. Teresa contributes a great deal by introducing us to her unlikely guides and teachers. *Mending Broken* will guide you to your own light and then you'll shine it for others too."

—Durga Leela, BA, CAS, PKS, RYT-500, founder of "Yoga of Recovery" www.yogaofrecovery.com

"Teresa B Pasquale has written a profound and profoundly moving book. If you have endured a trauma or know someone who has (that's everyone, I should think), you will want to read *Mending Broken*. Teresa takes you along on her journey, a path that has had genuine horrors, but a journey that, with help, emerged into light, love, and a future."

—Dr. Deborah Lee Prescott, PhD, author of *Imagery from Genesis in Holocaust Memoirs: A Critical Study* + English Professor at Palm Beach Atlantic University

"Teresa B Pasquale has written a beautiful human story of terrible trauma, suffering and redemption. I am moved and inspired by her courage, sensitivity and wisdom. And enlightened by her brilliant new focus on the process of healing, the importance of spirit, of yoga, of the body, of creative process, and of first establishing safety and coping tools and only then revisiting the raw traumatic experience in words."

—Dr. Nancy Coyne, MD, Psychiatrist, Yoga Teacher, + Equine Facilitated EPONA Provider

"This book speaks to the phases of trauma in a way that is so beautiful and exact. Teresa B Pasquale is clearly a talented writer, and artist. *Mending Broken* will be on your mind long after you're done reading it. Teresa has held the space for healing and never let go once she has her awakening. Bravo, Teresa! I'm deeply grateful for the lessons learned in your book."

—Shelley Rosenberg, author of *My Horses, My Healers*, + Equine Facilitated EPONA Senior Staff, www.myhorsesmyhealers.com

"This is a story of one woman's journey from trauma to triumph. Teresa B Pasquale has shaped her recovery from trauma into a way of life, both personally and now as a psychotherapist, from the inside out. She shares how she created coping skills that she now passes on to her clients and that she continues to apply in her own healing."

—Dr. Sally Valentine, PhD, LCSW, FAACS, Trauma Therapist and Certified Sex Therapist + yoga teacher, www.drsallyvalentine.com

"Teresa's depiction of her journey from darkness to light is powerful and genuine. Her poignant description of her personal trauma is enlightening to me, both as a mental health professional and a trauma survivor. I believe Teresa's simplicity of expression and her raw description of personal pain will be most beneficial for those of us seeking to heal ourselves and others.

> —Cheryl Young, LMHC, Clinical Director at Delray Recovery Center, www.delrayrecoverycenter.com

Teresa takes the subject of PTSD and clarifies what it is, how the brain behaves during the trauma, post trauma, and how it can heal. To say that this book is an altruistic endeavor is putting it lightly. It is raw, honest, and loving. This book is written for the victim, the clinician, and anybody who needs to know that somebody out there cares. It is evident in every page that Teresa does.

> —Michele Emerick, author of *The Climb: My Journey Out of Darkness and Despair*

Teresa Pasquale's book draws the reader in to a deep and tender place that speaks to our common vulnerability in her unique trauma. As we are drawn in, and just when we begin to reflect, she pauses in the narrative to frame what is happening in clinical terms and with imagery that gives the reader a window on PTSD, on the divine, and on life. Allow yourself to be drawn in, and as you engage you will learn not only about the issues of PTSD, but about yourself as well.

> —The Very Reverend Kathleen P. Gannon, Episcopal Priest, St. Paul's Episcopal Church, Delray Beach. Florida

"Every once in a while you come across an exceptional soul, dedicated to lighting the human spirit with hope and healing. Teresa B Pasquale is such a soul. Her words are worth reading for anyone who has entered the darkness and is looking for a flashlight of grace."

—Rabbi Jenny Yosefa Skylark, JD, author of *Terrible and Wonderful, Ugly and Beautiful Story of My Life So Far* and founder of Angelic Judaism and AHAVATAR Empowerment Therapy, www.rabbijenny.com

mending broken

a personal journey through the stages of trauma + recovery

teresa b pasquale

foreword by Michele Rosenthal, author of
Before the World Intruded

Request for permission should be sent to:
Teresa B Pasquale at
tbpasquale@gmail.com

Cover and book design by Teresa B Pasquale
Cover photograph (c) istockphoto.com/xxmmxx

International Standard Book Number (ISBN)
ISBN-13: 987-1480292741
ISBN-10: 1480292745

Printed in the United States of America
FIRST EDITION

This is a work of nonfiction. The events and experiences detailed herein
are all true and have been faithfully rendered as the author remembered
them, to the best of her ability. Some names, identities, and
circumstances have changed to protect the privacy and/or anonymity of
the various individuals involved. Others have vetted the manuscript and
confirmed its rendering of events. Also, while I am a therapist, this is
not a therapeutic manual. This is a personal account of trauma, PTSD,
and recovery by someone who has professional knowledge of the field
of PTSD, but is writing from the space of a survivor, not a therapy
professional. There are many resources which specialize in the
scientific/psychiatric explanation of trauma, PTSD, and healing. I urge
anyone who reads this text to continue their research and understanding
in therapeutic resources and access mental health providers in their own
area, as needed.

Dedication

To my parents, who loved me in all times and gave me a safe space whenever I needed it. To my sister, whose bravery and kind heart show me grace in the world, and in my life, always. To the many friends and kindred spirits who have been the sermon I needed, when I needed it, and the blessings in my life when I was too weak to ask for blessings. To the strangers who showed me love and the clients who shared with me their sacred pain. And, finally, to my husband, Chris, who is always my mirror of honesty when I need it (even, and especially, when I don't want to see it).

"...When two people have become present to each other, the waiting of one must be able to cross the narrow line between the living or dying of the other."

—Henri Nouwen, *The Wounded Healer*

CONTENTS

STAGE FOUR: Battle Scars

mending broken

Foreword
Michele Rosenthal

The most difficult aspect of dealing with trauma, addiction, mental illness and emotional pain is the way it sets you apart. You see the world differently than others. You find discomfort in situations in which others find joy. You lose language while others chatter effortlessly. You feel nothing in moments in which others shimmer with feeling.

Because you feel separate and apart, because it's difficult to connect and form meaningful relationships, you recede from the world seeking relief in the comfort of isolation.

The problem is that isolation only brings more unhappiness. Its darkness reinforces that you are worthless, undeserving, less than, and even utterly powerless. What you need in such moments is an element that is often in short supply internally but can often be found externally in the voices of others on a similar path: Hope.

As a trauma survivor who struggled with all the emotional pain of post-traumatic stress disorder for over twenty-five years I'm no stranger to what it feels like to be separate. My own journey toward the life of meaning, purpose and joy I now live was hard fought.

On the healing path another survivor offered to me, "When you lack your own hope, borrow it from others."

So that's what I did. I researched and read and looked for people whose lives presented enormous challenges. I studied how other survivors, in the truest meaning of the word, learned to pick up the pieces and put back together the puzzle of who they were. I learned a lot from a variety of sources.

In stories, memoirs, films and poetry others' voices gave me the courage to imagine that I, too, could find some inner resilience, put one foot in front of the other and trust that I could discover a way to mend what had been so horribly broken in me.

The healing process was not pretty and it took quite some time. I made many mistakes, lost friends, upended a career and taxed my most loving relationships. Eventually, however, I did accomplish what I set out to do: I emerged from the darkness of overwhelming emotional pain and reclaimed myself and my life.

Without the voices of others I'm not sure I would have known how or even if I did deserve to attempt such a daunting task. What I gleaned from the process is how enormously critical other voices can be in your own individual healing journey.

In *Mending Broken* Teresa B Pasquale offers a beautiful, honest, raw and proactive voice of hope.

By charting four universal aspects of life's challenges – their occurrence, aftereffects, recovery and moving forward – Teresa shows how, yes, we can be broken by things that are out of our control. But, yes, we can heal and reclaim ourselves, too.

In her story of survival, acknowledgement, pain, strength and courage you will see just how far down your mind can take you, and also just how high it can be inspired to reach. If you are on a journey to find relief from the emotional pain with which you live, I encourage you to borrow hope from Teresa's example and allow her voice to enter your darkest moments like the most radiant shaft of light.

In Teresa's words you will find not only hope for how you can move past your past but also a strategy easily adapted to your own private process.

In so honestly and publicly sharing her story, Teresa enters in, and contributes to, an enormous community of voices building a healing space.

It's in this space that we learn to reclaim connection to others and also to ourselves. Reaching out of your isolation, in whatever tentative, slow steps feel appropriate to you – whether it's reading this book or finding others with whom you feel comfortable enough to speak – can be the first step in building the life you most deeply desire.

In my work I am in constant communication with people seeking mending from around the world. Watching their processes, which span cultures, races, ages and religions, I've translated one of the most important lessons I've learned into a single, simple sentence:

"We don't heal in isolation; we heal in community."

By picking up this book you have, at this moment, entered a very wonderful community. Until now, perhaps, you have felt alone in your experience of guilt, shame, compulsion, fear, anxiety, panic, regret and a host of other unwanted emotions. In this instant, however, understand you have company in that space.

There are many of us who travel and have traveled the same road. Teresa's clarity and insights are a wonderful guide. As you read this book, allow its message of hope to wash over you.

I invite you to imagine how your life might change if you were to, as Teresa so successfully did, find a safe way to let your inner world out and the outer world in.

Following Teresa's example you, too, can find your path to freedom because you have enormous healing potential. The goal is learning to access it.

You can do this. Dig deep. I believe in you.

Michele Rosenthal
November 26, 2012
www.healmyptsd.com

Introduction | Stories from the Edge

I thought about writing this book many times, for many years. I am a bit of a perfectionist; it's part of my genetic code. As a result, the book began and stalled at about page forty many, many different times.

I thought about writing a clinician's view on my experiences. I considered explaining all the technical nuances of trauma from the inside out. Then there were times I thought about writing a memoir, cataloguing every inch of my own trauma and recovery.

In the end, the most authentic model of storytelling for me was a hybrid of the two vantage points and the two parts of my self.

I am someone who has studied the nature of this beast we call Post Traumatic Stress Disorder (PTSD) from every angle voraciously—as therapist *and* as survivor. I worked my way through text after text studying the nature of trauma and the brain to understand the what, why, and how of my own (and others') experience.

I am a survivor, beyond and before all else. That is where my journey began. Long before I studied the mechanics of the disorder—and long before I even knew that there was a name for what stagnated my life for over four years—I was just another person surviving inside PTSD. The disorder lived in my guts like a live virus—eating away at my self and my life. It ravaged every facet of joy and hope I once had, leaving nothing but bones and scattered remains.

Many people (professionals included) *still* say trauma can't be mended and there is no recovery from PTSD. I am someone who came out the other side of impossible. There is a vacancy in this field, it seems, of voices who have come out of darkness and can give the personal proof of healing.

In my recovery I poured over books to understand the disease that had once eroded my soul. I searched to find understanding and a way to dissect what seemed overwhelming down to edible bites. I *needed* to know, for me. Understanding was key in my recovery and a powerful tool for anyone who suffers and is lost. I hope that my experience can serve as a resource to those that wander and are lost in emotional pain.

Not everyone gets PTSD after traumatic experience. The generally recognized statistical average is twenty percent. Twenty percent of *all* people who experience trauma will suffer from PTSD. There are many theories why some people get it and others don't such as: the amount of social support a person has post-trauma, how immediately they begin treatment for their trauma, whether someone has had previous traumas, the inherent strength of a person's resilience, and innumerable other factors.

There is no definitive way to ward it off and for those of us in the twenty percent it affects us profoundly in one hundred percent of our lives.

I broke down my story from traumatic experience through the states of active PTSD and into a process of healing into four distinct *stages*. Each stage illustrates a part of the post-trauma experience which I found in both my life and the lives of numerous people I have met with a history of trauma and PTSD.

I am sure there are a number of ways the post-trauma experience could be parceled out. This is my version.

Each of the four stages begin with an introduction. The introductions describe each stage in palatable everyday language and discuss the nature of PTSD and the ways in which it manifests itself in a person's life—mind, body, and spirit.

I try to make my explanations as jargon-less as possible because I have found that the clinical language of trauma often shrouds true understanding of the nature of the emotional disease called PTSD.

After each stage's introduction I share short stories which bring into focus my life, its traumatic nose dive into PTSD, and the subsequent recovery process.

Some of the early parts of the journey are ugly, painful and gritty just as is the beginning of *all* brokenness.

As you continue through the timeline you will find increasing spaces and places where light shines through pain. Incrementally, hope is found poking its way into the darkened tunnel of brokenness and sewing together a mended self.

I hope this formula—part information and part story —will prove useful to a wide audience. This is a book on trauma for anyone and everyone: people suffering in brokenness, loved ones of those who are living in emotional darkness, and anyone who wishes to learn more about the process of trauma, PTSD, and the genuine potential for recovery in *every* life story.

Prologue | Bringing to Birth

Every second, minute, and hour of the day human life begins. Tiny purpose-driven molecules and the zygotes of zygotes find their way in the universe making up what we call life. This pattern has repeated itself for millennia. Throughout the history of our human existence on this planet people are brought to birth over and over again. Each human life breathes its way into the world fresh and shiny and new. This is our clean slate start.

Somewhere along the way hurts begin to form, sometimes small, sometimes large, and the rings on the tree of our life become full of divots and gashes. There are spaces in the plot of our lives where the path becomes jagged; the clean slate becomes full of chaotic and frenetic marks. Occasionally, time freezes completely, halting our individual universe and stilling the spin of our personal orb.

Somewhere, in the space after birth and preceding death, we are injured. Some of us are fractured and fragmented in such a way that whatever was born into our self—that fingerprint of being which defines who we are as a unique creature—is broken.

Mending broken is no easy task. It can take years for a human to be mended, sewn back together and reborn, and although we can be healed and we can find peace we will be reborn a new self; a self that remembers the breaking.

✸ Setting an Intention

The intention of this book is to follow the course of trauma from its origin to its resolution, insofar as we can "resolve" trauma. The resolution entails healing from the symptomology that makes up Post Traumatic Stress Disorder (PTSD), but we don't resolve memory.

Nothing erases what has been but we can learn to address the response system ignited by traumatic experience. We can recalibrate the response that flips a switch in our brain when trauma occurs which sets in motion our "survival mode" autopilot. This system *can* be repaired.

We can relearn joy, safety, love, comfort, and peace. We can find a way out of pain and suffering into grace and meaning. Sometimes meaning is found in understanding that, "This terrible thing happened to me, but out of it I can find a way to care for others who had terrible things happen to them."

Meaning can often be about gifting grace back into the world; the grace that was freely given which allowed you to survive and later to thrive after pain.

This new understanding doesn't validate that bad things *should* happen to good people, but recognizes that bad things *do* happen to good people. We have to resolve our denial of that fact to allow ourselves the freedom to find compassion and see grace in a world where that fact *is* true.

We, the wounded ones, who survive and later thrive, are sent back into the world changed by being broken. We are also uniquely capable of being guides with the roadmap home from brokenness. We have the chance to be what Henri Nouwen calls "the wounded healer."

I hope this book can provide some of that re-gifting of what has been given to me.

❁ Neuroplasticity

Humans are profoundly resilient creatures. There have been recent revolutions in the study of the brain and science of the mind which birthed a term to describe resilience at a neurological level. The term for resilience found in us at a biological level is called "neuroplasticity" which means: the brain can change.

This new scientific understanding and revelation of our cognition explains how the brain changes in the aftermath of traumatic experience. It illustrates the chemical change from normal functioning into an active state of PTSD which leads us to process the world in a chaotic and dysfunctional way.

However, the brain's complexity and cleverness is even greater than we give it credit for; even the brain's change *into* dysfunction represents a series of finely tuned responses meant to protect us.

Neuroplasticity also means that the brain can change *back*. More accurately, the brain can change *again* out of PTSD and into a new complex series of responses which allow us to move beyond survival mode into something new.

The way I explain neuroplasticity and the nature of how the brain engrains patterns of thought and behavior and can be just as capable of changing them (even those deeply imbedded and long-standing) is by asking people to imagine a racetrack.

Imagine you have run around the same racetrack all day every day for years. You can imagine this race track as your "normal" pattern of thought and behavior which precedes the storm of trauma.

This racetrack creates a groove in your mind and, over time, that groove gets deeper. Soon you are running in a hole.

When traumatic experience happens and the survival mechanism is switched on it is as if the brain has been bounced off its original track of "normal" and into an entirely new track (of self-protection).

The brain begins to run on this track, over and over, all day every day for days, weeks, months and years. The new groove gets deep and over time you are running that track in a daze, stuck in the groove of that hole your brain has dug with its survival response.

In this process from "normal" to PTSD your brain has already exhibited its ability for neuroplasticity to take place because it has jumped tracks from what it did before trauma to a new PTSD track after trauma. Unfortunately, the PTSD track is much deeper than the pre-trauma track and much harder to change.

There is no sudden bounce of the brain *out* of the PTSD track, like there was *into* the trauma track. We have to work very hard to climb out of that hole and build a new track to run on. Neuroplasticity proves that even though this is difficulty to do, it *is* possible.

Each time we are triggered and intentionally employ a different way of responding to the trigger we are slowly beginning to build a new track for our brain to run on. Step-by-step we begin to dig ourselves out of the deep hole of PTSD. We are creating a new racetrack.

Knowing this brain secret is important because as a person goes through the stages of trauma and recovery there are many moments of doubt, fear, hopelessness, and authentic darkness. Understanding the mind's ability to change can help us to push through the dark moments of the trauma journey and retain the possibility of light along the road to recovery.

In challenging moments there is one word which is a reminder of the freedom accessible to each mind, body, and spirit trapped on a PTSD racetrack—neuroplasticity.

The brain can change! Imagine the endless potential in that one short statement.

From when we are born to when we die, we have endless opportunities for rebirth. We *all* have endless chances to build a new racetrack and climb out of the hole of an old track that no longer works.

❀ The First Person View of Trauma + PTSD

My experience with trauma and PTSD is as a primary source. I am a survivor and was long before I accumulated any other titles of identity.

I am also a psychotherapist. As a therapist I have studied the nature of the brain and body in traumatic experience, after traumatic experience, and into the symptoms of PTSD. I have also studied and implemented—for myself and others—a myriad of practices for healing PTSD including: yoga, meditation, equine facilitated therapies, nature-based and creative arts therapies, traditional talk therapy, gestalt/psychodrama techniques and many other modalities of healing.

This book is a brief look at the petri dish of my life in trauma, PTSD, and recovery.

In some places I will take on my clinician's role to explain the nature of trauma and its impact on a human being.

In most places I will explain what trauma looks like from the inside as a person who lived down a rabbit hole for years, running a track of dysfunction. I will tell my journey out of that darkness and how I found *my* roadmap to a new "normal" and a personal homeostasis.

I often tell people trying to heal from PTSD that our path to individual wellness is like a fingerprint—all our stories of coming back to life have distinct personal differences. That said, the nature of the beast is very similar across the board. The symptoms and the stages of healing in my life, and in the lives of many others I have worked with as a therapist, follow a similar general course of recovery.

There are four stages which are outlined in this process. Each stage has a title page which integrates the metaphor of being broken and sewn back together. The introduction titles more accurately depict what happens in the process itself.

Below is a list of each stage title and introduction title in sequential order:

1. **Scotch Tape + Band Aids** | Brokenness and Slumber
2. **Ripped at the Seams** | Painful Awakenings
3. **Sewn Together** | Facing the Darkness
4. **Battle Scars** | Baggage + Letting Go

These four stages are my compartmentalization of the four emotional places on the roadmap from traumatic experience into a birth of a new self: mind, body, and spirit.

STAGE ONE

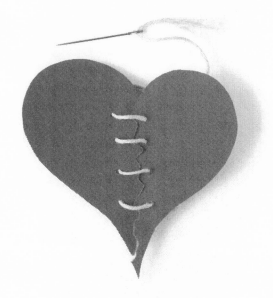

Scotch Tape
+
Band-Aids

Introduction | Brokenness + Into Slumber

When I started my work as a trauma therapist a longtime professional told me, "All we do as trauma therapists is put Band-Aids on open wounds and hope they stay on. We are really just trying keep infection out of the wound."

It took me a long time, professionally and personally, to believe that more than Band-Aid living was possible. During my own Band-Aid stage I never thought that there was anything on the other side of my semi-infected reality. I assumed the chaos and messiness in my brain was the new homeostasis for my life.

After my trauma I *was* held together with Scotch Tape and Band-Aids. I lived as a soul widow. I was a hollow vessel that moved and acted and functioned like a person but with nothing functional on the inside. I was a mess of guts and pain and blood which I tried to hold together with rudimentary tools.

The wounds of trauma are invisible. They are a secret no one knows carried by warriors on the front lines of their mind. The battle wages incessantly and exhaustively; it is impossible to see and difficult to heal.

When my clients come into therapy after one or five or fifty years of living in the Band-Aid stage I tell them to be easy on themselves. They can't judge their own experience or feel guilty for the time lost in the vacuum of crisis-stabilization.

They survived.

I ask that they give themselves credit for their own survival because to survive is an immense feat. The constant battle is exhausting and just to get through it alive is laudable. I remember the internal war.

I ask them not to judge how long it took. We must acknowledge the human strength in survival.

Stage one of trauma and the aftermath is just a matter of surviving—from one day to the next and one week to the next however possible. A person's focus is on keeping the guts and pain and blood on the inside, by whatever means necessary.

✸ Survival Mode

Our human brains are highly complex and heavily animalistic. The mind is the entity that helps us survive in traumatic experience and the same mechanism that can lock us indefinitely in trauma-response mode *after* a trauma occurs.

This is essentially what PTSD is: the trauma response triggered and then remaining stuck, like a switch you can't turn off.

I could talk about adrenalin, cortisol, serotonin, and all the hormones and chemicals that the brain produces to save us in dangerous situations, but the easiest way to explain what happens in trauma response is by looking into the animal kingdom.

The deer in the forest perks its ears when leaves rustle or twigs crack knowing that, as a prey animal, they are constantly at risk of being something else's dinner. A deer's natural state of being is in some level of vigilance. They have a heightened awareness of their surroundings and are always ready for any possible attack.

When the rustling leaves reveal another creature the deer will often freeze in place, trying to make itself invisible so that a possible predator won't be able to see them.

If the rustling figure in the distance begins to approach in a predatory way the deer has two options— stay frozen or run. They may choose either one depending on the deer and the situation.

As humans we do the same thing and, if necessary, a third or fourth option gets thrown into the survival response equation.

The primary survival mechanisms we employ as humans in dangerous situations are: fight, flight, freeze, submit.

Recent science has begun to discuss an additional response which is being called tend/befriend and enacted by the hormone called oxytocin which a mother emits in response to their infant. Essentially, it is the caregiving hormone. Some say this response of the body and brain can be attributed to the domestic violence victims who feel compelled to return, again and again, to their abuser.

A person who has suffered trauma and whose survival response switch has been triggered and stuck in place continues to respond like the deer in the woods. Their body and mind are always prepared for danger and prepared to respond with one or more of the survival mechanisms.

Unfortunately, since the switch is triggered and not turned off, reality is often seen through very distorted lenses. Everything and everyone can appear dangerous. The person in active PTSD is constantly responding to the world around him/her like the deer being encroached on by a predator.

In survival response mode we constantly react to people and experiences with fight, flight, freeze, submit, or tend/befriend. The world becomes a jumble of crossfires, misfires, and misperceptions. All of life is seen through the funhouse mirror of trauma.

Not only is it exhausting to live in survival mode but it makes for a very limited life experience. If you are lucky, you can manage the basics of a job and maybe a few casual acquaintances but the fullness of life is inaccessible. Years of a person's life are spent responding to everything and everyone as if it were a predator.

Much like addicts in recovery who "lose" the years of their lives during active addiction and have to restart life at the place, stage, and age where they began using drugs or alcohol, trauma survivors finds themselves losing time.

All the years lived in active PTSD are a jumble of raw emotions covered with heavy armor to protect from any possible danger without any real forward momentum. At best, a person can coast through life in a lateral place, but during the active PTSD experience there is no room to grow inside the self or in relationship with others.

The years of active PTSD are as blurry as a long night of heavy drinking, punctuated by acute moments of panic.

It's survival but a bare-bones survival.

During this time survivors are just trying to stay alive and not let all the guts and blood of pain pour out.

As the survivor, you are keeping yourself shut off and shut down, with only a thin layer of Scotch Tape and Band-Aids holding you together, and living one small rip away from complete collapse.

In the Grass

Something in my gut told me not to go. Maybe it was his voice on the phone. Maybe it was the hour of the night. All I knew was that my belly was churning.

I had broken up with him the week before and promised we would stay friends. So, when he called at 2 a.m. asking to meet up and "just hang out" I felt an obligation to comply. I hesitated for just long enough to feel the urge to say no, but he reminded me of my promise and I agreed to go.

I snuck down the driveway while my parents slept and walked one block over where he picked me up on the side of the road.

My gut was screaming, but my guilt was louder.

Some elements of the night I remember very well but much of the timeline is blurry. That is the nature of traumatic memory; full of vivid snapshots surrounded by fog.

I am pretty sure I was 18 but I may have just turned 19. I think it was fall but I can't be certain.

I do remember the dew on the grass at that time of night. It tickled my toes and saturated my skin with heavy drops of condensation. The tall grass licked at my legs as we made our way across the deserted park to the center; it felt ominously silent. He paused at the center of the field and laid out a plaid fleece blanket. He called me over, patting the plaid felt coating the grassy earth, and asking me to sit next to him.

I remember the frogs and the crickets in the background; their high pitch concerto rang in my ears. Their full insect and amphibian orchestra complicit to the crime only by proximity. They played their part in the unraveling of my life as the soundtrack to my undoing.

There was a moment when all I could hear was their music and all I could feel was the dew. When he grabbed me and held me down on the soft fleece covering hard earth I could feel my spirit begin to flee and my heart throb in panic all the way to my head. The pace of my heartbeat was a percussive patter joining in with the symphony of nature's music.

My voice began pleading, almost reflexively, "No, stop." I could hear myself saying it in an

unconvincing and useless kind of way. I already knew
he wouldn't stop before I began to beg.

He was so heavy on top of me. The air in my throat
almost completely stalled out halfway to my lungs.
My pleading had stopped and my breath was only a
whisper through my lips.

I needed to separate myself. I didn't want to feel it
anymore.

I began to feel light and untethered to the place on the
blanket and the man with his heavy body and heaving
breath. I began to float away from the ground and the
heavy rocks digging their way through the blanket
and into my head. I became un-embodied; floating in
the airspace above the dirt and away from the
ugliness of my violation.

I told myself:

*If I barely breathe, if I just stopped talking, it will be
over soon. Then, maybe, I can go home.*

All I wanted to do was get home.

Somehow, in that moment when my life broke apart
and all the me bled out into the grass, the crickets
kept on singing.

When he was done he rolled off of me with a
sickening grunt like a wild thing done with its dinner.
He got up unceremoniously. He was so casual it made
me queasy.

I think he started talking but I was mostly gone. His voice, his presence, his lumbering body hunched over as he rolled up the blanket faded into the background. He was just noise, like the crickets and the frogs.

And my legs were still wet with dew.

The only thing I remember clearly from what he said as we walked back to his car was, "You're not going to tell people I raped you, or something, are you?"

I shook my head. I pictured my bedroom and my mother. I just wanted to get home and so I kept shaking my head.

I thought:

If I can just get home everything will be all right.

Except it wasn't all right. Not when I got home. Not when I took a shower so hot it scalded my skin. Not when I went to sleep, or woke up the next day.

Something had left me. Something had drifted away in the mist above the early morning dew. Whatever was left of me was hanging onto life by a thread.

Whatever was left would just survive, and not much else, for a very long time.

The Aftermath

Living life in partial slumber is a disorienting experience. Time takes on a different quality and it's hard to distinguish things like days, seasons, and even what happened, when.

In the aftermath of my rape my life became cluttered with internal and external insanity and chaos. The world was unbearably bright and loud and scary. I have tried to do much detective work over the years. Many times I have tried to excavate and unearth the details of the four years that followed the night in the grass, but I have never been able to discern many facts. Every from that time has been distorted by the lens of suffering and trauma.

There are certain landmarks that are clear. One in particular I couldn't forget as much as I wished I could. It branded me with a mark of trauma deep enough to solidify my fate for the next four years of my life. It was the experience of my second rape. After my first assault I was standing at a cliff of emotional annihilation, almost daring the universe to push me off the edge. All I needed was one good shove to disappear.

In the rubble and artifacts of my life stands two clear incidents. My first rape and then my second which I have excavated in full from the archeology of my soul.

They are the only identifiable remains of a personal history lived out of focus while my brain ensured its own survival and protection through any means necessary. Between the first rape and the second I was a half-person existing in a half-life. After the second assault the sum of my parts equalled pervasive PTSD.

While the symptoms of PTSD are meant to build a wall of self-protection often the instincts of protection can skew the lens with which we see danger. We see danger where there is none and miss the red flags which a fully conscious person would see. My gut was no longer an accurate guide and I was living blindly.

I felt so pathetically typical after my second rape. I fell victim to the statistical data that says once you have been assaulted or abused you are more likely to have it happen again. It's like you suddenly have a

Lo-Jack that only predators have the equipment to read. I couldn't see it was there but then again I couldn't see much of anything.

The second rape was in Seaside Heights, New Jersey—one of the many places recently washed away by Hurricane Sandy. I can't say that some small part of me still remaining from that time, the part of me that hated Seaside, wasn't in some way purified watching the pier wash away.

It wasn't a literal satisfaction. Looking at it literally, I saw Seaside as a community of like humans who, now, carried a commiserate brand of tragedy from that town into their lives. The sadness of shared loss is something I feel deeply as a fellow trauma survivor.

At a symbolic level, watching the water wash over the coastline, decimating the same boardwalk I ran down in bare feet, clutching my shoes, and following the lights and the ocean to my hotel, felt like a metaphor for what I wished I could have done at the time.

The second rape it was perpetrated by a random acquaintance I met during another reckless night of partying. At the time I was practicing what I will call obliteration therapy; a personal practice of inducing the dissociative-like state by drinking until I could no longer feel anything in my body or my mind. I had gone down the shore with a couple of casual friends. They were in the prime of their party-crazy youth and equal matches—in their normative 20's wildness—to meet the needs of my pursuit for numbness, which came from a very different source.

The first rape was a shock to my system. It took every belief I held about goodness and my naive idea that all people were inherently trustworthy and broke it to pieces. After my second rape I became rabidly off-kilter. I was filled with pain and rage I never wanted to know again and it kicked every survival mechanism into a fully locked position.

I had been coasting on numb since the first rape. I was self-medicating with anything and anyone that would distract my mind from the images of violation that assaulted me, over and over again, any time I was alone. The methods I used to try to ward off the nightmares were also the same ingredients that made me vulnerable to a second perpetrator.

My defense mechanism of becoming comfortably numb was what hooked up and turned on my personal Lo-Jack for predators. It sent my second perpetrator right to me; the clearest and easiest target in the room.

I was the deer and he was another predator in the wilderness.

In the moment I realized I was back where I started—captive in a different man's web—I wanted to destroy everything. I wanted to decimate that boardwalk, that town, and everything in it that held the traces and stench of my second rapist and his crime.

Lying there in a strange man's bed I could see myself disappear into the atmosphere above my body. This new skill for disappearing left its mark and became my brain's favorite escape hatch in scary moments.

In trauma lingo it's called "disassociation" when you float out of yourself and into the air above your life experience. This response originates in trauma and falls in both the freeze and submit category of survival. Often dissociation becomes a cognitive habit the brain uses after trauma to escape anything that feels like it might be dangerous.

In that moment it wasn't conscious, it was instinctual. Disappearing was one of the best ways for me to get by and survive. I knew the drill by now and it was fascinating how the playbook hadn't changed. It was my first rape set to repeat, the only thing new was the face. That, too, would fade from my mind in the wake of trauma; lost in the overgrowing weeds in my garden of memories. I blacked out his face the moment he climbed on top of me and I can't remember, still, what he looked like.

As a result, from that night forward his anonymity gave him the freedom to roam my life in the shape of all men. His faceless silhouette would form into a generic archetype for my future with men and created a generic mold I would put every man into.

They were all predators, crouching in the leaves, waiting for the right time to attack.

If I almost stopped breathing during my first assault I definitely learned to completely halt breath during the second. I asked him to stop. I pled. I said it over and over again like a mantra. Stop wasn't in his playbook and I knew from my own experience that they were futile words.

I remember hearing voices outside the window of his bedroom. It was summer and the heat in his room was sticky and moist, as was his body. His windows were open and through the breeze I realized all that sat between his crime and the front porch was a thin layer of screen mesh.

I could hear the porch-talkers right outside the window. I knew they could hear me. Their voices were crisply clear as if they were in the room with us. It was a boy and a girl, about my age. Their playful flirtation made me think they must have been newly dating. I could see their shadows move and heard their porch chairs creak as they continued with their banter only a bedroom-width away.

I was completely alone. Not just alone in that room, but in life. No one was going to help me. No one really cared. I had lived, previously, in a white knight fantasy, always believing there were heroes. My white knight faith shattered against the screen, and was quickly replaced with the archetype of the universal perpetrator. Everyone was my enemy and there was no such thing as heroes. White knights were for the innocent and I no longer fit that description.

I *knew* they could hear me, because I could hear them, but for everything about that moment that mattered, I was invisible.

My voice evaporated in the air carrying my soul, my faith, and my belief in righteousness with it.

Survival was up to me and only me. That's what those voices told me. The voices of that couple were so much more complicit to the crime than the crickets, but equally unchanged by my pleas.

After he was done he rolled off me in the way that only a perpetrator can, making even the act of leaving grossly insulting. He turned his back for a few moments as he reached for his clothes and in a groggy stupor—one part alcohol and one part dissociation—I grabbed my clothes, my shoes, and the doorknob which fell off in my hand as I escaped.

I ran down the boardwalk, chasing the lights which marked every few feet forward on the straight path alongside the ocean. I had splinters in my feet, and survival in my brain. I wished the boardwalk would wash away. Even more than that I wished *I* would wash away with the heavy froth of the waves and just not have to *be* anymore.

Relocation Therapy

In a live taping of an Indigo Girls concert recorded at the Red Rocks Amphitheater in the jagged hills towering above Denver (where I once saw Ani Difranco) the lead singer mused, "Time moves differently in Colorado."

I wouldn't know how that goes for anyone else but time in Colorado certainly did move differently for me. In my case, that was ninety-nine percent trauma and maybe one percent Colorado.

I had always wanted to live out west. I imagined myself as Georgia O'Keefe in New Mexico, painting the landscape over and over because I was just too captivated by the beauty of the colors to stop myself.

I hadn't ever really thought of Colorado. Before my traumas I was constantly telling people I met that I would be leaving New Jersey soon, probably for Taos, Santa Fe, or maybe Tucson.

After my trauma I needed to run and Colorado seemed far enough. I knew a girl from high school who lived out there and decided it would be a good home-base to start a new life. I was trapped in the wild frontier of my psyche; a ragged pioneer just trying to cling onto life in the harsh climate of my mind.

I thought moving would fix it all. I wanted my clean slate start and I didn't want to be within a thousand mile radius of anything that reminded me of my pain.

The first time I saw the Rocky Mountains building to a crescendo out of the plains of the Midwest I felt a trickle of what seemed like majesty fill my soul. I drove out of the cornfields, away from the Northeast, and into the Front Range. Something about the mountains' largeness made me feel a whisper of hope. If beauty could trump pain in this new life I was making, I thought, I might have a chance of crawling out of the belly of my traumas. It had taken me nearly two days and one hundred radio stations to drive my way into this new life terrain and I was restless for change.

I fell in love with Colorado right away. It was an unintentional and an unconventional kind of love for a girl from the metro area of Manhattan. If beauty *could* have trumped pain, Colorado is the place it would have happened for me.

Maybe it was the nostalgic fragment of a little girl that lived somewhere inside. The little girl version of me grew up imbibing John Denver songs and still remembered all the lyrics to "Rocky Mountain High." I loved everything about the state, and the town of Fort Collins where I unloaded my car, and my baggage, and laid down three years of roots.

I've said, in retrospect, "If I had lived in Colorado *without* PTSD, I think it is a place I would have stayed."

After I relocated I found a job a few towns away. Every morning I drove to work southbound out of Fort Collins towards Loveland where I had a daycare job at the city's hospital. I would get on the highway around predawn and drive into sunrise.

I was able to find gratitude in the early morning commutes and the crisp clear sky which was only accessible above 10,000 feet. It took about thirty minutes each way; just enough time to catch all the colors of sunrise and all the shades of sunset.

My time working in daycare was comforting. I was the toddler preschool teacher and all the little ones loved me. They were tiny morsels of untamed joy, completely untarnished by the harshness of adulthood. In their presence I felt safe and I knew I was able to return the favor. Every day I wiped fifteen bottoms five times a day and became pretty proficient at potty training and two-year-old conflict resolution. I could do the work, I loved the kids, and it didn't require me to have a four-year degree or be able to do any heavy lifting with my mind. It was exactly what I needed because my brain had been shredded by the shrapnel of internal war and I did't have the energy to make it work hard.

Loveland was a strange place to spend a couple of years (before I quit to go work at an optometric office). While I was working there the town was part residence for the high-end families that worked at the Hewlett Packard branch just outside of town and part quick-dying farm town, full of old saloons and semi-toothless cowboys. For me it was a fascinating cultural midpoint—between two worlds I knew nothing about.

I was neither weathered cowboy nor businessperson, and for both ends of the spectrum I was, still, just the babysitter.

Loveland did have one unique feature. Due to its name it was the largest supplier and mass-mailer of Valentine's Day cards in the country. Every Valentine's Day special orders would come in from each state in the nation, to be mailed out of this little old outpost at the nation's midpoint, so that when the cards arrived at a loved one's door, the postmark read "Loveland."

Not that I found much love in that land while I was there, although I could see that it was a place where joy and peace and love could be found. There was potential for bliss in the shadows of rocky peaks and in the slowness of time that the Indigo Girls articulated. There was love to be had if you were in the right state of mind to know where to look.

I guess that is anywhere regardless of altitude.

During that time of my life it wouldn't have mattered if I were in Loveland, Fort Collins, or Tahiti—I had no idea where to look.

I had failed out of college in New Jersey. Self-medication, PTSD, and attempts at a college education don't mix, in case you were wondering. When that last thread of connection with my life before trauma was cut, I fled to Fort Collins for a stab at what we call in the therapy biz "relocation therapy."

Quick tip: it never works.

Even though I had driven over twelve-hundred miles in my 1989 Mazda, somehow my ghosts followed me. An emblem of one of those ghosts sat in that Mazda until I sold it. Hidden in the center console—under trash and receipts and hair bands—was the doorknob.

It was the door knob I had turned so furiously trying to leave the house in Seaside the night of the second rape. It was the doorknob I clutched as I swayed back and forth on the boardwalk—using the stretch of ocean and lamp light to guide my way back to my hotel. I clenched it so hard it left indents in my palm.

Before I fell asleep, or, more accurately, passed out that night, I shoved it in my pocket. When I woke up the next morning I stuck it in the car's console, where it stayed, as some sort of masochistic reminder that bad things can happen at any time.

It was also a reminder that no matter how far I drove away from the rapes there wasn't anywhere my trauma wouldn't find me. Maybe it was the part of me that knew I couldn't run away that left the doorknob in the console as a physical reminder of the pain that never left me.

Emotional Masochism

Besides my doorknob I had at least one other overt but unintentional masochism. This came in the form of a relationship I fell into with a boy from Wisconsin less than a month out of New Jersey and into the mountains. We were like magnets of codependency waiting to collide.

He was from a family of alcoholics and when he drank too much he had a tendency towards rage. He also had heavy pockets of insecurity which led to a sometimes scary possessiveness and more rage.

I was hollow and lonely and, for the first time in my life, without anything or anyone that made any sense. I had left all the bad stuff behind in New Jersey but also anything good, like family.

I felt like nothing. I felt like I could disappear. I didn't want to be nothing and I didn't want to disappear. It was terrifying to think I could just slip away and float on the air of dissociation into nowhere forever. The fear of not existing flared my survival mode into full panic. Something instinctual told me that if I wasn't alone then I couldn't disappear.

Something else in me, almost animalistic, resonated with his rage. I had a desperate need for something to protect me. His largeness and possessive anger were like a lion's roar and made me feel protected. The combination of his nature and my PTSD inverted what I should have felt, which was fear, and made me feel safe.

So, we joined together. He had anger and a need for nurturing due to an abandoning mother and a volatile father. I had a yearning for family connection and an internal panic which was muted by his loud roar. All I really wanted was something to protect me from the bad things in the wilderness. I didn't have the strength to do it for myself.

We cobbled together one whole from two broken parts and tried to create some poorly made knockoff of a happy family portrait.

Three years went by and we had gotten a chocolate Labrador, were sharing a rented townhouse, and had just bought a white Chevy Blazer we couldn't afford. I had left the daycare and was working at the optometrist's office but I didn't have many close connections because of the isolationist nature of our codependency and part of my impulse to nurture away his insecurity and keep away the rage. We were, both, feigning the life we wanted while internally combusting.

It wasn't his fault, it wasn't my fault. I spent many years blaming him for the way we were but that was a fiction I told myself. We were just two damaged people trying to pretend to be healthy.

Three years, increasing fights with increasing intensity, and I could feel myself again, standing at the edge of a cliff. I was on the precipice of submission to this life I didn't want but was comfortably dysfunctional. Each day I was letting go of more of my identity and giving myself completely over to our disjointed symbiosis. I was lost and sinking deeper and deeper into the dark void of unhappiness we called home. I knew if I did nothing that this would be our life forever. Even in rampant PTSD I knew what we had was not much of a chance at a life for either of us.

Maybe it was the last shred of healthy survival mechanism or one small piece of self emerging—tucked away in some hidden pocket of mustiness and mothballs—there was something churning in that region of my gut that I had switched off over three years before. I knew, from somewhere deep inside, that I had to leave or perish.

I woke up one morning and the words I needed to say were center stage in my brain, repeating themselves over and over. Each minute I was awake they built momentum with their urgency. I left for work at the optometrists where I worked in the front office. All morning the words ran through my head, persistent and urgent and refusing to be ignored.

My boyfriend had called at lunch. He liked to check in with me in the daytime and the more tense our relationship got the more claustrophobic his insecurities and more persistent his check-ins. He could tell in my voice something was off.

He insisted I come home from work at lunchtime, I guess thinking he could envelop me in the reminders of our comfortable numbness if we were face-to-face. I didn't want to let go of the words, as afraid as I was of saying them out loud. It was my script and I didn't want to forget it.

I thought:

Maybe this is better. I can just throw the words out at him, like hot coals, and run back to work before I can change my mind.

The second he looked at me he knew. I think we both knew what I was going to say and that asking me to come home midday had just cemented the outcome.

"What is it? What's wrong?"

He asked with such sadness. His eyes pleaded for me to stop before I said what I wanted to say.

"This isn't working. We have to break up."

Even after the words came out I kept repeating them in my brain, afraid if any other thought made its way into my head I would take it all back. If I looked at the sadness in his eyes, or listened to the urgency in his voice when he told me we could still make it work, I would collapse. If I collapsed I would release the last bit of fire still left of the authentic me; held hostage inside this cage of PTSD melded with codependency.

"This isn't working. We have to break up."

I don't even really remember if I repeated a second time out loud, or just in my head. He cornered me at the top of the stairs and told me no one else would love me as much as he would. He threw the words at me like a threat and told me, in his desperation, that I would never have better than this. No one would ever love me again the way he did.

No one would love me.

I believed him. I felt completely broken and unlovable but even the prospect that no one else ever would, or could love me wasn't enough to make me stay. It had been so long since I had anything in my life that looked good, I only anticipated bad and worse in situations. I imagined myself alone and broken forever. Whether it was weakness or strength, I didn't really care. I had lived without happiness and if this was love I could live without that too.

My little morsel of active gut kept fueling the repetition of the phrase in my head, keeping me on track: this isn't working, we have to break up.

I said something about needing to get back to work and dodged his attempt to block the exit, fumbling for the keys as I rushed out the door.

Almost immediately after I got into my car my body began to hum with something new. It was something I hadn't felt for a very long while—fear. The feeling was potent and it made my body shake and my breath stall out. I was in a panic and I wasn't completely sure why.

In leaving the safety of unhappiness I would be alone. Alone was scary. Alone was where bad things could happen. It was much scarier than a life without love. In a life moving forward without him I wouldn't have my lion anymore and I didn't have enough strength for my own roar.

All the way back to work I shook and the rest of the day—breath nearly imperceptible—I kept reminding myself of my mantra. I willed myself to repeat it over and over, letting no other thoughts come in.

This isn't working. We have to break up.

I thought if I stopped repeating I'd take it all back. I wasn't sure I could do this living thing on my own. Being hollow, miserable and comfortably numb, I knew. Being alone, awake and open to danger was terrifying.

STAGE TWO

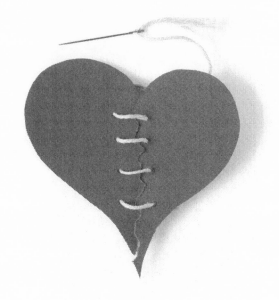

Ripped At The Seams

Introduction | Painful Awakenings

Waking up is hard to do. Not in the "it's 6:00am and I hate the morning," kind of way. In an excruciating and frightening kind of way.

In some Christian sects there is this jargon for that "come to Jesus" moment which certain Christian people refer to as the moment a person is "saved." They consider it a fixed and singular point where all bad exits and all good enters. I always had a hard time, linguistically and spiritually, with this simplistic explanation of salvation.

Neither life, faith, or trauma fit into that constrictive, tiny package.

We all have rumbles, pops, and bursts which make up the incremental and erratic fireworks of life and shine light into the darkened and ugly places. Some we recognize and some we don't. Some come from an internal source and some from an external source. These moments are ***all*** salvation moments.

My salvation moments—when I was given glimpses of feeling and living again and I shed the first layers of skin in my PTSD recovery—were excruciating. I call them painful awakenings because that is what they were. They were a series of experiences made up of various sparklers and firework lights, that felt like giving birth and the labor pains of waking up were emotionally unbearable.

Most people I talk to who have suffered from trauma, addiction or issues of emotional despair relay similarly painful moments and experiences.

All of our lives are punctuated by moments of clarity. We all have those microcosmic awakenings to a part of ourselves which previously lay dormant.

In the case of PTSD, the traumatic experience puts our bodies and minds into a state of shock which then creates a necessary numbness. Its counterbalance—the awakenings from numbness to consciousness—is like a death and rebirth process.

Imagine a body being resuscitated from the brink of death. Visualize the image of a defibrillator trying to shock life back into the nearly lifeless. These are the birth-pangs of awakening and this is what it feels like to wake up from the slumbering and numb stage of PTSD.

Sometimes the pain and shock of this kind of awakening can be so acute we want to go back into the cocoon of protection we have built around our heart and mind and soul to protect us, keeping us in that numb place.

The devil you know is better than the devil you don't.

Wanting to stay in the comfort of one's own devil is hard to resist. Inside of my PTSD numbness I was getting by. I was surviving. To make the decision to leave that place took more energy than I thought I had in me.

Slowly and episodically little shards of light began to peek through into my cave of security and safety. The light cast from a shockwave surge blasted into the heart of my pain. The experience was similar to pinholes pricked into a darkened box. Each hole cast a little speck of light into the darkness, illuminating more and more area in the box. The light flecks cast shadow in the box. The scariest thing about light in a once darkened box is that you begin to see the monsters in the corner.

When this process happens to someone with trauma and PTSD their mind slowly becomes illuminated. Memory and emotions are activated and that includes fear.

The new light takes adjustment for eyes not used to the brightness. It creates an emotional flinch and an urge to turn away until there is enough time to adjust to the bright color of life and to begin to look at the shadows previously left discarded in the darkness.

Painful awakenings feel like tiny pin holes of light in the dark. At first they hurt but if we can let our eyes adjust we can begin to embrace the nature of light *and* shadow, and balance the two.

The Veil Tears

After I broke up with the Colorado boy strange things started to happen. In my cocoon of dysfunction, inside a possessive relationship which was full of our mutual messiness, there was safety. An unseen, unidentified, and unconscious safety found in having someone always with me. At home and going out into the world there was that feeling of having the weight of a man, my roaring lion, with each step I took.

Once we broke up I was alone and alone in a way I hadn't been the entire time I had lived in Colorado. Part of me began to realize why I—the person who had avoided relationships for my entire adolescence and early adulthood—had gravitated towards one so quickly when I moved out west. I was petrified of being alone. Every step into my new solitary life left me vibrating with a sense of doom.

I had started back at school, quit the optometrist's office, and taken a part-time job selling make-up at Clinique. Even in this small piece of my new beginnings there was a tint of absurdity because I had never worn makeup. I had no idea who I was and I was grabbing blindly at anything I could hold onto.

The numbness I had worn like a cloak for over three years began to peel away and everything underneath was raw and torn apart like rare meat that had been left to wild dogs.

I was afraid to go to my car at night, scared when someone came up behind me, and I was always looking over my shoulder.

My first semester at Front Range Community College was so painful. I was using my brain for the first time in years and it wasn't used to the workout. Like all under-exercised muscles, my brain hurt from the use of previously flabby parts. I felt old and out of place. I was one hundred years more soul-weathered than all the perky eighteen year olds on campus. I had no idea how to relate to their life experience and wasn't about to share mine.

I cringed when people talked to me, disoriented by the bright sunlight peeking into the darkness of my closed emotional box.

It was painful to pretend to be normal especially because I had no idea what normal was supposed to look like. All around me there was the buzz of youth and enthusiasm void of the taint I carried with me every day. I didn't trust the benignly friendly Colorado smiles of all the peppy, happy young people enjoying their young lives.

There was a part of me that envied and hated their capriciousness with the full poison of venom. There was a part of me that thought:

How dare they be so light and free and unburdened by one hundred years worth of ache. How dare they not know pain and live so unencumbered by fear and hate and vacantness.

Then one afternoon I was sitting in the requisite "Human Sexuality" class which fulfilled one of the general requirements and remember hearing the professor say the words *date rape.*

I hadn't expected it, and my newly acute system, full of hair triggers and trip wires went off like a land-mine. I felt shakes rippling through my body's core and limbs, and chills began running concurrent with sweats as my face flushed and my breath quickened.

I thought I was going to scream, but instead I found myself walking towards the door, then speeding down the hall, and slipping into the nearest bathroom stall. I collapsed onto the floor for five minutes that felt like an hour. I was a puddle of panic: shaking and crying and hyperventilating.

As absurd as it may sound, this was the first moment I thought:

Something has to be wrong with me, this can't be normal.

Years into dysfunction—still not even thinking about the term PTSD—and for the first time I knew I needed to talk to someone and figure out what was going on.

Empty Chair

While I didn't want to consider Post Traumatic Stress Disorder as the root of what was going on inside of me, I had finally identified and admitted to myself that traumatic experience was what had led me to flee the New York City Tri-State area. After my panic attack in class I knew I couldn't ignore it anymore.

I had no idea what the next step was but meeting with a therapist seemed like a logical idea.

I searched around to find someone who treated trauma, was on my insurance, and was a woman. When I found one I scheduled an appointment.

I thought about canceling or not showing up every day until the appointment arrived. Sitting in the parking lot minutes before I was supposed to walk through the therapist's door my highly protective numbing and denial system tried to tug the key back in the ignition and make me drive away.

I wanted to face the devil I didn't know and see what he looked like.

I was afraid all the time and so tired of the internal war. I had the wear and tear of a thousand years of fighting. I was petrified but I was prompted forward by the more imminent need to know what was going on with me.

Before that point there had been five people I had told my trauma story to and each of those five experiences pushed the word rape further back into my mind and out of my vocal cords.

The first person I told after my first assault was a mutual friend of my perpetrator and myself. I can still remember his response and how it elicited, deep inside of me, both nausea and flinching pain. We were on his porch sharing a beer. It had been a week since the rape and I had come to his house specifically to tell him what happened.

I don't know what I expected. Maybe validation. Maybe empathy. Maybe revulsion in him at the fact that he could have ever been friends with someone who could do such a horrible thing.

"Do you know what he did?"

I asked him with an earnestness that was still so naive, certain he would say no.

He replied, "Yeah, he told me. That sucks, but it's over right? So what can you do?"

Then, within in a blink, he went back to smoking a cigarette and swallowing the last of his beer.

The second person I told was a girlfriend of mine. I came to her after the second assault. I had given up on the idea that a guy would or could understand the experience but I was looking for something in her that I hadn't gotten from that man I once thought of as a friend. I still wanted validation, empathy, revulsion—something.

Her response was, "Yeah, that happens sometimes. It's happened to me too, but you just have to move on. It's not worth thinking about it. It doesn't change anything to think about it."

Before I could even pause for shock, she had moved on to other topics of conversation.

The last three people I told were all guys I had hung out with after both assaults happened. They were, not so subtly, pushing the encounter towards hooking up and the last thing I wanted to do was get physically intimate with anyone. I told them about the rapes as a sort of plea to back off and take it slow, thinking it would keep them at bay.

Each one's reply was the same, in the same order, with almost the same wording and inflection:

Part one: "That sucks."

Part two: "Do you want me to kick his ass?"

Part three: "So, we're still gonna hook up, right?"

We did. If I had learned one thing— besides the fact that people no longer gave a shit about rape—was that saying no was a futile waste of valuable breath. I learned through my rapes that you never say no. PTSD had given me the coping mechanism to escape even when escape wasn't possible: dissociation. So, I learned the only way to deal with men and physical contact which was to disappear. My sexuality became vacant and so did my body every time a man touched me.

After that I went completely numb—emotionally *and* physically—for all those years that followed. Nothing touched me, nothing could get even close because I just locked away the hurt and any sensation, including and especially emotion, that could leave me vulnerable.

As my long-cultivated veil of self-protection—which I had built so high—came crumbling down I had no back-up resources. I had no idea what to do with feeling things again. I needed some kind of help.

With a deep breath and limp faith I walked into the therapist's office and sat down in one of the two chairs in front of her desk.

I think she must have gone through a brief family history and then asked me what brought me in that day.

My trauma story came flooding out in vivid color and terrible clarity. Every little detail came like a waterfall in hefty waves of visceral experience and unedited emotion. I told her everything from the dew in the grass in Maplewood to the sound of the couple talking on the porch outside the window in Seaside.

After I finished we sat in silence for what felt like forever. I hated it. My brain drowned in silences. They were as scary as the dark.

She leaned forward and pointed to the chair next to me.

"Talk to that girl that you were when those terrible things happened. Tell her it wasn't her fault."

"It wasn't your fault," I said, barely glancing at the chair, as if I was ashamed of the ghost sitting next to me.

"Tell her it wasn't her fault," she said again in the same even tone.

"It wasn't your fault."

"Tell her again."

"It wasn't your fault."

She made me do that exercise at least ten times. Then she turned the chairs to face each other and asked me to talk to my "inner girl" with kindness and empathy for what she had to go through.

I complied. Trauma survivors are often pretty compliant. Compliance is another method of survival. Don't struggle, just agree; there is less chance of getting hurt that way.

I can't remember what I said after the exercises. Tears flooded my eyes, shame and self-pity sat restlessly in my gut, making me want to vomit. All I knew was I needed to get out of that room.

I was just waiting for the permission—compliant as I was—to get out of that room.

When she finally let me leave at the end of the session I spent a long time in my car outside her office waiting until my hands stopped shaking so I could grasp the wheel to drive.

Years later, as a therapist myself, I remember learning this same "empty chair" technique that the therapist used with me (or against me) back in Colorado. It is a powerful therapeutic tool from Gestalt therapy. In my own professional practice I have used it sparingly—probably more cautiously and sparingly than most would—because of that personal experience I had.

In retrospect, knowing what I know now as a professional in the field, I find that therapist's tactic borderline unethical and definitely unsafe.

Even outside of my particularly cautious scope of practice, when it comes to that Gestalt technique I don't know of any ethical or safe trauma provider who would implement the "empty chair" technique in the first session with a trauma client. To use that technique before rapport has been built and before a client obtains the safety tools for self-soothing is a great risk to their mental stability.

Sadly, many of the best lessons I have learned as a trauma therapist have come at the cost of myself or someone I know being victim—in a new and painful way—to trauma work done in dangerous ways.

I add this note both for survivors to understand that I do not think that was a viable way to further unearth my already raw emotional state and for professionals to understand it is not something I would ever recommend in a first session.

I think it is important, as survivors, to be able to know that we can speak up, listen to our gut, and walk out of unsafe spaces, even and maybe especially when those are therapy spaces.

I think it is equally important for therapists to know the power these therapeutic measures can have on the raw and exposed souls that walk through their door. I hope all therapists can carry the responsibility of being a trauma therapist with sacred and special care.

Midnight With the Lights On

When I got home the night of my overexposing therapy session I drank half a bottle of wine to try to calm my body down enough to get to sleep and when I finally knocked out I knocked out hard.

I woke up and the bedroom was so dark. All I could see were the shadows of my unearthed ghosts and all I could feel was the thud of my knees as I flipped out of bed so fast I didn't have time to brace myself for the fall.

I whipped my head around in every direction as the shadow of my own silhouette played tricks with my fear on the walls.

When I flopped out of bed I didn't know where I was but I was certain someone else was with me. I had the sensation of some heavy, lumbering, foul breathed man hovering over me. It felt like his body was pressed against mine, as I lay on the floor, stunned and paralyzed. I could feel his heaviness crushing my ribs and pressing down on top of me. Even as I became aware I was exiting a dream state, and the reality of being alone on the floor by my bed began to settle in my mind, I still felt like he was in the room. I felt like my ghosts had pressed their way out of my inner darkness and come to life.

I hadn't been ready to go into the dark corners of my mind and pull all the guts of my trauma out—not so spastically and abruptly. I didn't know what to do with it now that it was out. I had no idea how to contain it and no way to stuff it back into the shadow boxes.

All I could see was the outline of this man, lingering, like an imprint from my past in the darkness.

And I couldn't stop shaking.

I felt insane because I knew no one was there, yet I felt watched, surrounded, and suffocated by my own memories come to life.

I ran through the apartment turning every light on like I used to do in my bedroom when I was a little girl. I remembered one summer in elementary school reading too many chapters in *101 Scary Stories to Tell in the Dark.* I woke up with that same feeling like the monsters had come to life, but that was different. That was a child's fantasy built from an overactive imagination and a naive misunderstanding about what kind of monsters *really* existed in the world.

The last light I turned on was in the bathroom. In that room the feeling of being watched was so intense I couldn't even look in the mirror. I was afraid of my own reflection staring back. Part of me thought if I looked in the mirror long enough the large man's face would reappear, standing behind my reflection. Then he would swallow me up into nothingness, pulling me into the darkness of my nightmare like my personal Freddy Krueger.

I spent the rest of the night on the bathroom floor near the doorway. I was low enough to the floor that I didn't have to look in the mirror but intentionally positioned so that I could see every doorway in the rest of the apartment. I wanted to be ready in case someone came out from the shadows where light halted and darkness could swallow you whole.

Risky Living

After the therapist visit and the night spent on cold tile, I spun out a little bit; more than a little bit. I didn't want to feel but I couldn't turn the faucet off—memories were leaking out of every side of my brain and spilling into the land of the living.

I pulled back from my social circle and began spending many nights at home in the apartment with a bottle of wine, DVDs of *Sex and the City*, and all the lights on. All I did was watch back-to-back episodes of the show, drink wine, and yell at God until the dawn light came peeking through my vertical blinds, the moths had gotten tired of fluttering over the balcony light in the apartment I shared with no one, and I was out of cigarettes.

The *Sex and the City* compulsion was mostly about being homesick. The wine was an attempt to shut the doors to the past and numb out the present. Staying up all night—as long as the lights stayed on—meant no time spent in nightmares or in the shadows with ghosts. The yelling at God was new.

There were two things I hadn't done in the three plus years following my traumas and it wasn't until I started doing one that I realized both had been absent for so long. I hadn't had any kind of conversation with God and I hadn't written a single creative word.

I had done both practices, religiously, from the first minute I learned how to pray and write until the day I was first raped. Returning to this part of my self I hadn't accessed in years created a new level of pain and awakening. I found myself in the early dawn of many mornings with God listening patiently to my tears and verbal beatings, all of which were aimed in His direction.

He took everything I had and carried it along with me. He sat night after night watching my soul crack open and then carrying it, and the rest of me, into every dawn. He never left my side.

Sometimes She was gentle, Her voice soft and maternal, other times He was stern and harsh and blunt. Whatever I needed to get me through that night—whether it was a smack or a hug—God was the arbiter of my pain.

When the emotional pain was at a peak, in the time right before dawn where it felt like night couldn't get any darker or longer and I was so tired of fighting and fueled only by rage He would shout at me (sometimes with expletives) in the voice I needed to stay alive.

In the early dawns, when I was tired and my voice was hoarse, and my cheeks stinging from too many tears, he would gently hum me to sleep, wrapped in the love I desperately craved and reviled. Through all the tears, amid the smell of stale cigarette butts piled in the ashtray, and an empty wine bottle by the sink, for days that turned into weeks, I knew He was there.

I can't explain why or how I knew it to be true but I felt His presence. I needed His presence because without it I lingered too long in dangerous and intolerable silences.

This was where my adult relationship with God began to take shape and—in the years following—I would envy those nights. It took immense patience and contemplative practice to get that intense presence back. Even then it was just flickers of light, not the whole bright white inferno of God.

In the absence of everything else—in the void without hope, strength, joy —I felt Him most. It was enough. It was enough to keep me alive and find rebirth in the rubble of my own pain.

Then—when I was finally tired of the forced insomnia and the hangovers, the hacking cough, and the lonely vacant life—I got up off of the floor of my living room and decided I needed to go back home.

I didn't want to run away any more; besides, it clearly hadn't worked.

STAGE THREE

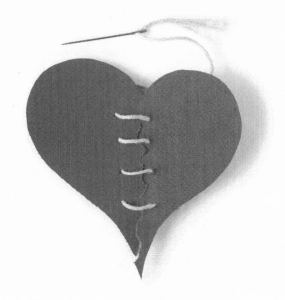

Sewn Together

Introduction | Facing the Darkness

Everyone's path to healing is like a fingerprint.
Each one of us carries distinct DNA for our healing
process inside of us and there is no one-size-fits-all
method of recovery. Different things work for
different people at different times. The more trauma
survivors I meet who have suffered from PTSD the
more ways to heal and patterns of the healing process
I discover.

There are certain elements that usually find their way
into the mix due to the nature of how the brain, body
and spirit hold trauma. There are certain avenues we
can take to healing that give us opportunity to access
each of these parts of the self but there are a number
of treatments, tools, techniques and practices which
can take us into the space of recovery.

The same way one person is a more visual learner,
another more cognitive, and another more somatic,

some of us are more visual, cognitive, or somatic in healing.

In addition, given the variables of accessibility, opportunity, and awareness on our own path to healing a person may gravitate towards one mode of healing first simply because it is available. Then they may discover other methods further along on their journey.

We know traumatic information is contained in the mind which is where we process memories. This is, also, where our subconscious tucks away the fragments of things that end up in our dreams, and sends signals to the body system telling it how to respond to situations in an animalistic way. The animal nature gauges how we assess the safety or danger level of our environment.

First, lets address the nature of memory function. I could talk about the amygdala, prefrontal cortex, and the thalamus but this isn't that kind of book. There are plenty of great books which describe neurobiology in detail but I want to describe what happens in a way that is a bit more visual.

When I speak with my clients I explain the way our brain processes memories by asking them to picture a card catalogue. Bear with me—it will make sense.

Our everyday mundane memories—the good, the bad, and even most of the sad—are processed and reconstructed out of the three-dimensions of living experience into something flat, like an index card.

The flat card is then filed away in the card catalogue of our mind. Our brain can always recall the history of our lives as needed but unless directly called upon to do so it doesn't really bother too much with the past.

When trauma occurs and the brain's survival mechanism kicks in it halts the everyday memory process, holding the traumatic memory in a brain-limbo where it isn't condensed down into a flat card *and* isn't filed away. The traumatic experience stays stuck in the forefront of our mind like a three-dimensional movie clip only one tiny hair trigger away from being re-ignited. When it is triggered it returns to us in an instant either through a visceral flashback or a horrible nightmare.

This is why when a traumatized person is triggered they say it feels like they are right back in their trauma in every sensory way possible. The movie clip replays in three-dimensions and you capture every sound, sight, touch, taste, and smell of your trauma whether the experience was five minutes, five years, or fifty years ago.

This process will continue to happen until the trauma is dislodged, processed down into the flat paper card, and filed away with all the other memories.

✸ How We Heal: Mind + Body

While we have our own distinct fingerprint of healing there are specific parts of our self that have to repair, mend, and integrate for healing to happen and recovery to begin.

Emotional wounds and traumatic stress engage all parts of the self: mind, body, and spirit. Those of us on the pilgrim's path to recovery have to engage *all* these parts of ourselves at one point along the journey to find the peace that comes with healing and reintegrating a *whole* self.

The processes of the brain and body are innately linked. The messages from the brain trigger responses in the body and body experiences trigger memories in the brain. Each end of this chain reaction has to be addressed but I learned something interesting along my path to healing, first sensorially, then academically. While we think we need to access trauma from the brain first, talk is not necessarily the first way we can or should engage the traumatized system.

I spent a couple of years going to a single individual session with therapist after therapist, repeating my trauma story, feeling flooded in all my senses by retelling my trauma and in response leaving the session and never returning again. I repeated this process over and over again for at couple of years, not understanding why the intensity wasn't dissipating and I couldn't sit still long enough to stay in therapy after telling my story.

Then I found yoga, and in yoga I found breath, and in breath I found something I never had in my hit-and-run therapy sessions. In the practice of yoga and the application of yoga breath I regained a capacity for calm and the ability to breathe again.

This is the point I am going to focus on one clinical term and discuss the part of the brain called "Broca's area" which is the language center of the whole mind operation. This little fella, Broca—which we need for so many all communication throughout our lives—is our go-to resource for communication. It is also the part of the brain which shuts down at some point in the traumatic process. For me, talk shut down each time I floated out of myself into dissociation and fled the scene of my perpetrators' crimes.

What happens each time our traumatic memory is triggered—and that three-dimensional movie becomes a living experience again—is that our brain goes back to trauma-response mode. When our brain goes into trauma-response mode language becomes difficult and sometimes impossible.

Which is why for some people accessing the brain's talking center may, first, require some kind of somatic or body-oriented practice including but not limited to: mindfulness, meditation, yoga, tai chi, and breath work

Another great option can be found through engaging in relational-based therapies which are foundational building blocks for trust by engaging in a relationship with another person place or thing. These, also, may not require talk at all such as: nature-based therapies and animal-based therapies (dogs, horses, and even dolphins) as well as creative arts therapies. All these engage the relational experience and acting-out what is felt without having to engage in talking about it.

All these techniques and practices become tools for the toolkit that can give us a place to return for safety when we need to calm down. It can also be a way to regulate our mind/body experience so that we don't have to live inside the trauma every time we are triggered. It also provides the support necessary so we can be ready to do the talk therapy and address the cognitive—thinking— element of trauma recovery at some point in the future.

This is not *always* the first step on the path to recovery and its not every person's fingerprint formula, but it was mine.

I think it is important to understand the nature of the brain regarding speech, be able to name the space called Broca's area and learn its quirks, regardless of which path to healing you walk.

Whether you begin or end with talking about your trauma, as a survivor there is no such thing as too much information about the nature of PTSD. Information, in trauma recovery is power, and we need all the power we can gather if we want to find healing. It is a tiring trek on the pilgrim's path to recovery.

✸ How We Heal: Spirit

I am not one to dictate faith but I will say with full certainty that we have to recover our faith to find healing. That said, this statement can mean many different things for different people.

In traumatic experience we lose faith: in ourselves, in others, in the world at large, and down to the microscopic level in all minutia of life. We lose a grip on things like purpose and meaning. How can we find meaning in a life and a world that would do "that terrible thing" to us?

One of the first books I read as a trauma therapist was one of the most profound in helping me regain my spiritual self and begin to heal from that most important and existential place—trying to find meaning out of horrors.

The book was *A Man's Search for Meaning* by Victor Frankel and if you ever want to *not* feel sorry for yourself read his account of a man who made it through Auschwitz and found meaning through his experience and a deep understanding of the holistic, spiritual and deep abiding nature of love and grace through and in all things. He realized that even, and maybe especially, suffering carries inherent meaning which we can learn from and grow from and find a way back to beauty.

His struggle to find meaning is as reassuring as his finally finding it. He reminds us that it *is* a struggle to regain meaning in a world where horrific things can happen to good people every day. In the case of Auschwitz horrific things happened to an unconscionable amount of good people every day. Victor Frankel found meaning out of his horrific experience and founded a psychotherapeutic concept called logotherapy as his response to this existential idea. Logotherapy is now known as one of the founding theories of existential therapy and psychological thought.

While his book is a bit technical in certain places the premise and the conclusion are ultimately philosophical and spiritual. I recommend it often to my clients.

We have to believe in *something* for life to be worthwhile. For me that something is God and in saying God I mean, also, the God in everyone else and the God in me.

One of my favorite Franciscans, Richard Rohr said: "My deepest me is God."

Learning and relearning to love myself and other people, finding trust in the smallest of places, and building that trust outward and upward, allowed me the spiritual freedom that my traumas had stripped away from me so many years before.

I am not here to tell you what *your* faith should be, or how it should look, only that I genuinely believe faith is a core essential component of the trauma recovery puzzle. This piece of the puzzle fits alongside the integration of healing in the mind and the body.

I have had many clients say to me over the years that they don't believe in anything. I ask them if they can name one person or animal or place that they love implicitly and completely.

We all love *something*. We all have faith in something and we have to start from that place to find our way back to any wider-reaching faith.

Start with the beach where you had your first kiss, or your grandparent who hugged you so tight it made you feel warmth and love from head to toe. Begin with your dog who may be your most loyal friend; licking your tears while you cry.

Start with something—anything—and faith will blossom in *that* place and begin to grow everywhere else.

Water it, feed it, nurture it, and faith *will* grow.

As faith grows, and love grows, meaning will begin to return. It won't be meaning that eradicates the terrible things that happen, or that makes them okay, or even necessary. It *will* be a meaning that gives us the capacity to live in a world where bad things *can* happen, and *do* happen, and still find love and faith and grace.

I am who I am because of every element of my life and, yes, trauma is one of those elements. Can I answer the question, "If you could do it all over again...?" No. But I don't have to because this is the life I am in and in this life some bad things happened. My particular bad experiences have informed every part of my life since they occurred and will continue to do so if I choose to let them teach me.

The bad things are what led to me being in a PTSD stupor for four years. The bad things are the reason I am a trauma therapist and they are why I write these words in this book.

This is my life. I cannot choose or un-choose what has already happened but I *can* choose how I react and engage with the world going forward.

I have found in my post-PTSD life that faith is much stronger and more powerful than fear or hate or bitterness or anything that opposes it.

So consider what you love and believe in that one thing. I promise it is a doorway to a new beginning.

Writing + Fighting

When I realized that the two things I had
stopped doing in my life of active PTSD were talking
with God and writing, and when I decided to move
back home and finish up my bachelor's degree from
the comfort of my parents' warm and healing nest, I
knew I wanted to study literature and write again.

I had always vacillated between English and
Psychology majors in my first go-around at college.
When I returned to school I knew I needed to find my
voice before I could even consider listening to anyone
else's. My English Major was the easiest choice I had
made in a long time.

I had to write. Before my traumas and PTSD writing
had been my everything. It was all I did when I
wasn't reading. I was winner of the most books read
over the summer in Mrs. Paciga's 2nd *and* 3rd grade
class. That's right, two years running, which got me

the only prizes to the only races I'd ever win in the shape of two gift cards to "Do Me a Flavor." The winnings were as deliciously sweet as winning.

I paired my English Major with a Women Studies Minor and inside this blended curriculum for my undergraduate degree my authentic self began to re-form; clumsily at first, then veraciously, and then at such an intensity it was almost ferocious.

I had decided to not be afraid anymore. It was a conscious choice. Fear felt powerless. As I began to rebuild from the remains of my former self, in the space where woundedness had happened, I began to reclaim a bravery I had lost along the way. Crawling out of my personal darkness and finding my way back from years lost into a tunnel of fuzzy memories I became determined to never be weak or afraid or hurt again.

The further away I got from the girl who sat on bathroom floors weeping and shaking the more disgusted I was with her. Every part of her sickened me—her smallness, her incapacitation, her blindness. I began to feel rage. Rage was an extreme emotion I didn't know how to contain and it began splattering, messily, all over the place. I had rage at those who had hurt me, rage at myself for being weak and for losing so much time, and rage at anyone I saw in my life who I felt were enemies of my newfound independence and strength.

I could no longer understand that person I had been. She was a sad fiction I had created. She was a myth.

Then she actually became fiction as I wrote story after story in my writing classes about this girl who was stuck in terrible situations. I would look down on this girl from my new and powerful stance, feeling so far from her. I didn't even understand who she was and, without fully admitting it, I deeply resented that she ever existed.

I felt like she had wasted so much of my life. So much time was lost and so many years had been carelessly spent that I could never get back.

Out of that rage and denial I created a new kind of armor to keep all the strength and individualism and power I could gather intact. All I wanted to do was be unbreakable and impenetrable.

I quickly became enamored with feminism. It was an easy sell for a young woman looking for strength and aspiring to strangle her weaker self right out of her life story. I tried to be an even-minded feminist, full of sound theory without a man-hating agenda. I tried really hard. However, my underdeveloped self and my own agenda got in the way of embodying any authentic kind of feminism.

I couldn't understand the Colorado girl but I also had no existing sense of self so I looked for a prototype I could mimic to feel genuine and strong and beautiful.

I read the histories of generations of strong and historically potent women. I wanted to drown the weak girl with their words.

What happened instead was that *my* feminism became drowned in rage and shame. It was diluted by a personal history full of archetypal men who hurt and took and controlled.

I decided to completely write those men and that weak girl out of my new life story. In rebirth I would be cleansed of needing them and I was sure I could shake the memory of them, given enough time. I was reviled by the idea of needing anyone, *especially* a man.

I would be Adrienne Rich or Bell Hooks or Gloria Steinem. I would be unstoppable.

I would never be the girl in the grass or the sad figure swaying home by the light of the boardwalk lamps clutching a doorknob. I would never be the woman locked in a mutually dysfunctional relationship or that heap of nothingness piled like old laundry and trembling on some bathroom floor. I decided that I was so far away from who that girl was that she no longer existed.

I was in control of my body and my mind, and no one would ever hold anything over *either* part of me again.

I read Jane Austen and Margery Kempe and Kate Chopin's *The Awakening*. I wrote papers on the nature of subversiveness in women of previous eras. I found women suffocated by the mores and ethos of their times who were full of passion and intellect and capable of verbal weightlifting on each adverb drenched page and in each poetic syllable. I focused on women who wrote their way to personal independence. I wanted to write my way out of my life as it had been and into something new and I was convinced if I looked close enough at the pages, in the space between margins, I would discover the key to my liberation.

In my Latina Literature class I learned about Sor Juana Inez de La Cruz, a nun from Mexico, who was one of the first published and accepted writers in the Latin world. She fought for the education of women and died in a romantic gesture of bravery caring for nuns with the plague. Ah, to die of the plague, I thought, what an honorable way to go.

I studied the paintings of Frida Kahlo and dissected the pain in her figures. She was intoxicating, in her fearless disavowing of feminine standards, and her self-defined sexuality of choice.

I devoured all these new definitions of womanhood.

My Brazilian literature professor spent one entire lecture discussing the phrase "come me" which, in Portuguese (and Spanish) means "eat me." He explained how it really symbolized a holistic consumption that was mind, body, and spirit.

I ate and drank the women of feminism and female figures in the history of literature. They were everything I wanted to be and I swallowed every morsel of their strength I could imbibe.

I wasn't them and I wasn't whole. I denied a part of me and in return fear found its way back into the dark places of my mind. The shadows crept into my waking life, through a loud noise, the touch of a man, the betrayal of a friend, or any circumstance in which I felt emotionally claustrophobic or trapped.

I couldn't see these women I idolized or myself in more than one dimension and as a result I couldn't become a fully integrated person.

I didn't know how.

I became some facsimile of feminism that wasn't really feminism at all. Feminism became a shield, more of a title than an action verb. I created a stringent personal code which I tried to use to build safety and strength for me in the world. Anyone or anything that didn't fit into *my* code was unacceptable and immediately discarded.

I was becoming very dogmatic. I was as rabidly dogmatic as I was ravenous for information to feed my dogmas. Paradoxically and simultaneously, I railed against systems that I thought purveyed rigid dogmas which at the time included: religion, patriarchy, marriage, and the American dream.

I became my own self-contained oxymoron. I created my own rigid dogmas and rules of life and if anyone crossed the line, violated my code, or was a part of anything that stood against what I saw as "right" or "just," through my foggy lenses of misguided intentions I threw it or them away.

I had wasted too much life and lost too much of myself at the hands of others. I wasn't going to stop for anyone.

I was an emotional bulldozer.

Being a bulldozer made me feel strong and safe and protected. I needed it to reclaim all that I had lost. It worked for a time to get me stronger and more independent. It helped me to learn what I loved and was passionate about again. I was learning elements of who my authentic self might be but my pursuits, in their rigidity, could only got me to a certain a point in my recovery and then—like all one-dimensional things—they stalled out.

It was more than survival but it wasn't a strong foundation for an integrated and balanced life.

Over time my new way of being left me feeling confused, conflicted, and hollow. If I lingered too long in the memories of the past I discovered there existed deep pockets of shame hiding in the corners of the remaining, untouched, and hidden darkness.

Resurrecting Teresa

One of my women studies professors had a very strange habit of insisting she was psychic. She would tell each of her students, in each class, which loved one or spirit guide was sitting or standing beside them during her lectures.

It was such a distracting characteristic that each class with her became consumed with us, like observers of a poorly run magic show, watching her "work." She would ask people—like a poor-man's John Edwards—if their grandfather had passed on, or was it a grandmother, or maybe it was an elderly angel that was the figure of someone's grand-spirit who resembled an elderly grandparent standing next to them.

She was usually so off-base it was hard to take her seriously but as if we all thought there might be a slim chance she was not just eccentric, but also a bit clairvoyant, we would glance over our shoulders when she honed in on the air above us or next to us.

Then we'd watch her eyes fall into an otherworldly trance and become lost in an awkwardly long silence.

One afternoon, at the end of class, I went up to ask her a benign question about a homework assignment. She paused, staring at me until it was really uncomfortable making me blink much faster and fidget. Right at the point of intolerable, when I began fighting the urge to look away she finally broke the silence with a question.

"Where did you get your name?" she asked, tilting her head sideways like dogs do when they are confused or intently concentrating.

"Well, I was sent to an orphanage after I was born, in Bogota, Colombia, and the nuns who ran the place named me after Teresa of Avila because I was born on her feast day. My parents kept the name because, by chance, my hometown church was St. Teresa of Avila."

I think that was the most I had ever said to her and as I finished my run-on sentence I reflected on my odd over-sharing and my unintentional verbal regurgitation of my name's full lineage. I wasn't sure why I replied in such detail.

Her head still tilted she said, "It wasn't by chance. There is no such thing as chance, Teresa. I really, really think you need to read Teresa of Avila's book, *Interior Castle*. I just feel that you need to read it. I feel like there is some connection there, something deeper than you know."

I nodded my head and mumbled a "sure" as I walked away, but her words lingered in me. It was like a Whoopi Goldberg moment. Remember that moment in *Ghost* when something gets turned on in a hiccup of the universe and Whoopi goes from being a storefront scam artist to a genuine psychic? It was sort of like that.

I don't know if my professor's hiccup moment lasted longer than that one interaction. By the next week's class she seemed typically eccentric and off-kilter. Either way, something in the way that she said what she said, and the feeling in my body and at the center of my chest when she said it, made me feel compelled to listen.

Even when I ignored the impulse for a week or two it returned like a ripple of fire in my body. One afternoon I found myself in Barnes & Nobles, running my fingers over titles in the "Christianity" section of the store, sneaking looks behind me every few seconds, like a guilty customer in the "X" rated section of a video store.

I wasn't sure if I had ever visited that section of the store before. My dogmas, at the time, precluded anything that looked like traditional religion. Religion felt like another kind of prison.

I knew God was there, in my life, from when I was little. I couldn't forget—even when I desperately tried to—how God sat with me on bathroom floors and through 4:00 a.m. tears as I screamed into eternity, rage-fully holding His name on my lips like a curse.

He watched me be reborn out of immense pain and in some way I was sure He helped to birth me. He had been like a cosmic doula, carrying me out of numbness and into a chance at life again.

Although I never talked about it with anyone else sometimes in the car, or in my bedroom at night, or in quiet moments in the school library, we would sit in silent conversation. He tried to be there for me and I tried to push him away. I didn't want to need anyone or anything, even and maybe especially, Him.

I didn't know how He fit in this new life of mine or how I felt about prescribing to anyone else's rulebook, definitely not religion's, but maybe not even God's.

I didn't want to give up control.

It was the only part of my path to healing that I had really mastered—being in control.

There I was, thumbing through the "Christianity" section, searching for something, but I wasn't sure what kind of something.

All I knew was the name of the book I felt I had to purchase, written by my namesake and recommended to me by a feminist psychic.

Teresa of Avila was someone I hadn't thought of for years and never really thought of at all until my professor asked me about her. Her name and the title bounced around my brain playing pinball and messing with my concentration. The name Teresa of Avila and *Interior Castle* kept pinging, periodically, between my ears. It was annoying as a fly buzzing around my head, close enough to hear, but too small to see clearly.

I grabbed the book off the shelf, if only to end the internal racket in my head. I started reading it that night and wasn't able to stop until it was done. Something mystic stirred in my soul; bigger than a fly, and more like the radiant wings of a butterfly. I didn't know what to call it or even that it was a mystic call but it kept fluttering calling me forth into further discovery of this new kind of faith experience.

People ask me when I became a mystic or "crooked mystic," to be more precise. I could say it was the night I read *Interior Castle* but I think my mystic origin story began much earlier. My odd professor's psychic spasm and my subsequent reading of *Interior Castle* awakened a sleeping connection which had been traveling with me since birth. My professor's one moment of clairvoyant clarity stumbled upon an *actual* spirit guide in my life.

I was born into Teresa and resurrected her dormant spirit the day that I read *Interior Castle*. Every moment since I have carried her, in varying states of consciousness and awareness of her presence.

I had never been able to find my birth mother and after years of searching in my early twenties through two private investigators, and a few dead ends, I finally realized that she would always be a mystery. First came grief, then acceptance, and then a deep understanding that my mother, not the one that bore flesh, but the one that birthed my soul, was always with me, and always would be.

Teresa of Avila, and the contemplative dimension that she gifted me brought me into another leg of my healing journey. This new curve of the path would open me to life outside of all dogma and give me a chance to heal the part of me I had not yet thought to repair—my soul.

Teresa's resurrection to me, and in me, was profound. It changed the direction of the rest of my recovery and drastically altered the roadmap of my life.

Breath. Faith. Meditation.

After reading Teresa of Avila I went on a quest for something more than just the words of others, or my own. The literary and theoretical studies of my undergraduate degree were good enough in getting my brain in shape and helped me create the cognitive foundation for my understanding of others and myself. After reading Teresa I was ready for a more experiential approach to my healing. This new dimension and my hunger for experience sent me looking for something deeper than the black-and-white world I had been living in.

I wanted what Teresa had found and articulated in her interior castle. I wanted to find and explore my *own* inner rooms and the many mansions of my soul.

I was a spiritually seeking neophyte and I was going to look down all accessible pathways to find some of that silence and bliss which Teresa had discovered in and with God.

In this search I discovered yoga.

In yoga I found the only physical practice of any kind that my body could do without twisted ankles and asthmatic panting. More importantly, yoga reconnected me with something I hadn't identified as lost—my breath.

Years frozen in numbness had taught my breath to stay held, reflexively, most of the time. Then, periodically, that breath-stasis would be followed by the rapid and spastic hyperventilation of panic.

All those years I had been tuned out to something so simple and essential to the human experience—breath. I had spent years not paying any attention to that lost relic of my traumatic experience. What a simple thing. How easy it was to break, and how long it had been broken without any awareness on my part.

Breathing in, arms rise, breathing out, arms descend, bending at the hips, and fingers fall by either foot. Upper body relaxes over lower body, then inhale, as the tips of the fingers touch the ground and eyes peek out through the fingertips, then exhale, head hangs loose as the body relaxes into the stretch. Then breath leading movement forward, inhaling again and arms sweep up. Eyes look up, and palms press together over the head. Exhaling, arms descend, back at either side of the body. Spine is tall, and you find rest in standing mountain pose.

My first sun salutation is something I will never forget. It was in that experience I realized there was so much more to breath than I ever knew. I was able to, finally, pull my body out of the past traumas where my lungs had been trapped. They had stalled out somewhere between freeze and flight. I was still breathing as if I was suffocating under the weight of a man's body. I had been breathing that way for nearly four years.

I found a freedom I hadn't ever known before in yoga. I also discovered an empowerment that defied my misguidedly militant feminism that wasn't really feminism at all. It had just been a method I used for personal control, to ward off the past and stave off fear.

In yoga I learned a way to manage fear *without* control. Yoga gave me tools that were alternatives to control.

Beyond just the breath of yoga I found freedom in the wave of movement, and this rebuilt my comfort in my skin. The comfort came slow, like the gentle flow from downward dog upwards, with a soft roll, vertebrae by vertebrae, to a strong standing mountain pose. In each class, with a softness and care for myself I had never accessed before, I slowly regained the comfort in my body. This was no easy task. I remember spending years wishing I could hide every inch of my skin with clothing, reviled every time I saw a man's eyes look up and down my flesh, nauseated by the thoughts I imagined running through his head. To love my body rather than carry shame and hatred of all my identifiable lady parts in its curves and hips and breasts, was something I did not come to easily. It took a year or two of yoga practice to begin to feel both beautiful and strong enough in my skin to not let men's eyes penetrate my healthy self-perception.

As I engaged more with my yoga practice I felt fluid and alive and beautiful. Yoga was where my soul could dance and exhibit that dance in unison with other souls, all breathing and moving and centering together. It was both internal solace and external community in a way that was completely unthreatening—and I wanted more.

One of the yoga studios I went to in Hoboken had weekly Buddhism classes taught by a Buddhist nun. It was a course meant for novices and westerners curious about the mystery and mystic avenues of the East. While I loved the asanas (postures) of yoga it was the breath and the silence that I knew I needed more of to regain some internal peace not derived from forced control of life circumstances. I was beginning to discover that letting go, rather than holding on tightly, might be more fruitful in my recovery—for my mind, body, and spirit.

Every Wednesday night for three hours and over the course of a year I learned the premise of Buddhist meditation in both scholarship and practice methods.

My teacher wore saffron, shaved her head, and reminded me a bit of Pema Chodron, except she was from an entirely different lineage. In my ignorance, until I started studying with my teacher, I had no idea there were so many different sects of Buddhism. The Christian mystic Thomas Merton had been fond of Zen Buddhism, the Dalai Lama practiced Tibetan Buddhism, Thich Naht Hanh has cultivated an amalgam of various traditions including integrating some western thought and psychology, Pema Chodron was a Shambala Buddhist, and my teacher happened to be from the Kadampa Buddhism tradition.

I learned about healthy detachment and love that could touch people in the space of silence. I learned about the power of communal quiet. I began to understand, at a level larger than myself, the possible ways, in meditation or prayer, to change the landscape of consciousness by changing the landscape of your inner self.

In our small windowless room below the Hoboken city streets we could make a ripple of intention and attention which penetrated the atmosphere around us.

I learned that one human soul, gathered together with many others, had the potential to grow intention into something larger than personal or theoretical ideals.

Focus and peace, begun inside, had the capacity to unfold a palpable collective wave. I learned that our collective wave of focus could change the emotional topography of our environment.

In the guided mindfulness meditations with my teacher—a classically trained clown turned receptionist by-day, and Buddhist teacher by-night—I also began to learn how to lead my mind into creating sacredly still internal spaces.

Sometimes we would be immersed into the imagery of deep pools of water where thoughts would bob or sink in the vast ocean. Sometimes she would take us into a forest full of the smell of pine cones where I sat in rich burgundy-brown soil breathing and clearing my headspace of clutter. Other times she took us to a wheat field with cloudless blue sky and eternally welcoming quiet.

I learned to control thought and feeling and breath in a way that required no aggression or hate or violence or shame—only acceptance without judgement, criticism or blame of self or others.

I didn't always get it right, and much of the time it was more struggle than silence, but at least I had the guidebook.

When I had found the path to stillness, self-acceptance, and a way out of the rage I had carried for so long—for myself and others—I began to find yearning again. The yearning tugged at me like a toddler who has to pee, at first a soft suggestion, slowly building in urgency. I returned to my image of the interior castle I carried with me, painted into my consciousness by my namesake.

I loved my yoga practice, and embraced my Buddhist meditation, but there was something, for me, that was missing. My one constant place of comfort through all the darkness and the light wasn't part of the linguistics of these worlds: God.

I wanted everything I already had with the allowance for God to be at the center of my overflowing cosmic wheel of ancient and mystic practices.

I realized that for my particular spiritual healing journey to progress I needed to explore—in the space of this newfound silence and peace—the God in my soul that had never abandoned me.

I was finally in a space where I could hear God more in the silences, but I didn't have a formula for accessing a deeper space of retreat with, and in, Him.

I wanted what Teresa of Avila had with and in God.

With a little research and some book-lending from my mother, I was guided to two men who radically changed my faith practice and spiritual path: Thomas Keating and Richard Rohr. Both men were Catholic priests from monastic orders—Fr. Keating was a Trappist monk and Fr. Rohr a Franciscan. Their teachings unlocked the doors of Christian mysticism and gave me the roadmap to a more intimate relationship with God.

Their teachings also revealed a practice that would become a large component of my life's work, both personal and missional—the practice of contemplative prayer.

In all the practices that led me to a space of rest and relationship with God, I had found so many beautiful spiritual gifts. Yoga returned me to my breath, and restored my connection and affection for my own body. Meditation was a conduit to finding stillness in my mind and releasing many of the pockets of rage and shame I had carried for so many years.

All of these elements stirred a fire in my soul, but alone they could not sustain the burn.

In contemplative prayer I had finally found the last piece of my mystic puzzle. I found a way to repair the relationship I had with God and find softness in my heart for His love of me. Finally, I had the clarity to see the full compassion and charity He had shown me in all the times I needed Him, even when I chose not to see Him standing beside me.

I began to accept and integrate these essential elements which I needed to progress in my recovery and on my mystic pilgrim's path.

I found acceptance for the fact that bad things happen to good people and understanding that God did not "make" them happen. I accepted with gratitude the awareness that in my darkest moments He *was* my survival, and forgiveness, and strength, and love when I did not have the capacity for any of those things. Whether I saw Him at the time, or not, He had been there.

My breath was back in my body and it was as though I could feel Him inside me each time we met in prayer. I could see how He breathed each breath of life into me daily. I saw how He had resuscitated my soul out of darkness, and gave me the gift of a spiritual fire that could and would *never* burn out.

STAGE FOUR

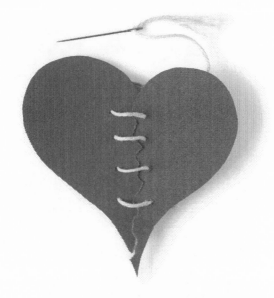

Battle Scars

Introduction | Baggage + Letting Go

My friend and colleague Michele Rosenthal and I keep saying we need to write a book on the post-PTSD experience. We want to create a survival guide for the maze of what happens when healing has taken place and recovery is in full swing. We both agreed that we had spent so much time researching and plotting the course of our recoveries that once we had shaken the shackles of PTSD we couldn't find any resources on what came next.

Post-PTSD recovery life, initially, looks a lot like the "White Rabbit" of "Alice and Wonderland."

"I'm late, I'm late, for a very important date. No time to say 'Hello, Goodbye'. I'm late. I'm late. I'm late!"

Not completely sure what I was running towards, or what I was rushing away from, as the fog of PTSD lifted I began to live life like it had an expiration date. It was as though I thought that suddenly something would happen which would shift me backwards. I felt, at any moment, I might fall back into a deep slumber.

It took me many years and a few good conversations in the early part of my friendship with my friend Michele to sort out this post-PTSD response. First, we communally recognized that we were both experiencing a similar impetus of unknown origin. Furthermore, we began to identify the what's and why's of it all.

What can I say, we are the Magnum P.I.'s of the PTSD experience (and the post-PTSD experience).

Although I am probably more rightly depicted as Inspector Gadget—accidentally stumbling upon the truth that was always right in front of me.

Once I realized the world wasn't about to disappear or, more to the point, that I wasn't going to disappear from the world, it gave me some time to step back and look at what all that post-PTSD mania had created.

Finish Bachelor's degree—check.
Finish Masters degree—check.
Get a job working with trauma survivors—check.

However, I hadn't yet figured out how to integrate the person that all those bad things happened to, who had fallen into the numbed-out slumber, with the highly functional—and almost disturbingly—over-productive new me.

The healed me just wanted to leave the other part of me behind. Even when I accepted and let the shame and anger go I didn't really have much use for the other me. This attitude left twenty-five plus years of my life dangling in the wind with nowhere to go and abolished any reflection back into the life history of the artist formerly known as me.

I was healed. Why go back? There wasn't anything of use there. I wanted to do, make, create, help!

Don't you remember?

"I'm late, I'm late, for a very important date. No time to say 'Hello, Goodbye.' I'm late. I'm late. I'm late!"

❀ Learning the Modesty in Recovery

What I had to learn from flopping and floundering on my way to important places is something that my brethren in a different kind of recovery—addiction recovery—knew all too well and learned from the very beginning of their healing.

Humility.

In regaining all of this authority, knowledge, empowerment and strength I had forgotten to retain anything that resembled humility. It seemed like a weakness I wasn't willing to test out, as though the bottom would drop out of my life if I lost control.

Again, addicts learn this fact so quick and get it so clearly in their recovery program. It is a genius of the 12-step program.

Blundering Teresa, doing my PTSD program my own way, needed many face smacks from life before I was able to learn the humility found in letting go. I mean really letting go. Which is not the same as meditating on the idea of it or sitting with it for an hour in prayer, but living the art of letting go.

It was then that I learned the secretest secret of all. Letting go also made way for the grace and true peace of giving up control.

Let go and let God. That's what the 12-steps tell us.

It was such a hard thing to do. I had no control for so long over anything, except how to numb my symptoms, that once I was in control of my life, my emotions, and my reactions to the world I wanted to hoard all the spoils of my conquest, and never let it go.

Even valid pride which comes from worthwhile endeavors—like surmounting many of the stumbling blocks of PTSD—can get in the way of the final parts of an *integrated* recovery and an *integrated* self.

I needed to learn and apply a few key elements in my life to becoming fully integrated. I think we all need to do that when entering the realm of our own post-apocalyptic self.

I needed to learn to slow down. Life wasn't stalling out again and I needed to learn there would be time to do all the things I wanted to do.

I needed to learn to find humility and let go of some of that hard earned empowerment long enough to see that I didn't have all of life figured out (and I didn't have to).

I needed to learn to give up control to a power greater than myself. I had to really understand and act from the understanding that I was not the God of my own universe, and when I tried to be, it never ended well.

And, I needed to learn that it was okay to remember the past, to be honest about what happened, and how I got to today, because that is all part of my personal pilgrim's path and *my* story of ***mending broken***.

White Rabbit Rebuilding

Even with the resources of yoga, breath, meditation, *and* contemplative prayer at my disposal it was very hard for me to really slow down. Actually, it seemed that as my recovery progressed and the closer I got to full PTSD healing, the faster my pace of life became and the more expectation I had for myself to do more, be more, learn more, and improve to the outer limits of my potential.

There was a lingering feeling of being in a dream I might wake up from and a fear that my clock on productive living was somehow going to run out.

I *was* Alice's White Rabbit.

The problem with productivity as dysfunction is that it reaped rewards and no one demeaned my hard work and quick progress. It was the epitome of the American dream.

In the eyes of everyone else I was just succeeding.

No one knew that under the surface my actions had nothing to do with an American ethos and everything to do with absorbing every moment of life to a dehydration point and sucking every trickle of juice out of the freshly squeezed orange that I called life.

Part of the issue was that I felt behind. I felt like I had to play catch up for the four years of living I missed. I was eager and engaged and passionate about everything I did. My actions were propelled by an awareness of how amazing life could be. I carried within me a deep understanding of the pain found in living inside an emotional fog.

In every way I felt late. I was behind everyone else's time clock and behind in my expectations of myself. I had been given a new chance at life and I didn't want to waste a single moment resting.

Life was intoxicating.

Learning brought expansive levels of understanding. I absorbed everything from literary fiction to books on the neurobiology of trauma. I went to workshops on everything from the mystic traditions to all manner of integrative healing modalities. All of it brought me an adrenalin feeling—in a strange way mimicking and engaging the same system of hormones and chemicals induced in trauma (adrenalin, cortisol, serotonin). Now, instead of inducing incapacitating fear, my high-octane hormones propelled forward a rabid lust for understanding the world, people, and all the many nuances of humanity.

Even as a child I was tenacious and excitable—always like a hound dog with a manic streak when I caught the scent of something that fascinated me. After PTSD, this kind of insatiable living became something of a self-imposed prerequisite for my recharged life.

I couldn't stop. I wouldn't stop. I felt accountable to make the most of being able to make it out of the trauma fog and I felt—at an imperceptible level—that if I paused for too long this whole thread of existence would disappear.

I felt like I might disappear, again.

I don't think I realized this wasn't just a personalized post-PTSD condition until I met my friend Michele. We were both bloggers at the time and found each other through the community of PTSD sites and blogs—running into each other in many a virtual corridor. When we touched base through email we found out that we lived within twenty miles of each other. At this point I had relocated from New Jersey to Florida; she had moved from New York to Florida. We decided to meet one steamy summer afternoon at, of course, a domestic violence event. After the event was over we walked and talked up and down Atlantic Avenue in Delray Beach until my flip-flops had worn blisters in between my toes.

That is when I realized, and maybe we began to realize mutually—like the PTSD detectives and trauma microbiologists we both were, equally teeming with tenacity—that after PTSD there was something else that happened. There was a whole new animal of experience beyond the rainbow of the almost mythic land of post-PTSD.

Considering many professionals and sufferers alike still thought—through a history of stigma and misunderstanding about the disorder—that there was *no such thing as post-PTSD,* it was no wonder no one was talking about what happened in this phase of recovery.

This white rabbit existence was something we realized even then that no one had ever really looked at, let alone talked about, and definitely not from the personal perspective of a survivor.

From my new relationship with my partner in PTSD crime-fighting I decided to again offer myself to the petri dish of my own experimentation to better understand this post-PTSD phenomenon and to learn how to find something I hadn't had since I was a pre-trauma kid. I was seeking a balanced self and a balanced life and something that resembled authentic joy. I was ravenous about living life, but I had trouble just being still in the moment and enjoying the space of quiet.

I was looking for a life that was not too much and not too little. I wanted life just right—to throw in a little bit of balanced living advice care of *Goldilocks and the Three Bears*.

Another one of the most difficult things for me to sort out was how to integrate my recovery self with all that came before recovery. I still hadn't figured out what to do with all the past baggage.

I felt like someone who had just lost hundreds of pounds. The fat was gone from my body, but what remained was stretched out sagging skin which had been over-flexed from years of being tugged on until it lost its elasticity. Inside I felt psychically healthy and emotionally fit but outside there was all this sagging skin with nowhere to go.

What was I supposed do with the baggage I didn't need to carry around anymore? What was I supposed to keep with me as a reminder? What skin did I need to cut away because it was surplus and what did I need carry with me in stretch marks and useable scars?

The further into my recovery I got, the more I realized that when we become well we don't erase memory. There are imprints of what came before but, like the flattened index card, the trauma experiences have found a place in the card catalogue of the mind. They have integrated with all the everyday memories.

All the same, even flattened, my traumatic memories carried more weight than the others. They were always going to be heavier than the everyday sads, mads, or glads of life.

I knew the traumatic experience *could* serve a purpose for my own life and for the lives of others. I just had to figure out what stayed and what needed to be released.

The Wounded Healer

Henri Nouwen wrote an entire book describing "the wounded healer" and detailed both the assets and the stumbling blocks encountered when you try to help others heal in the ways in which you have been wounded. It is as clear in his writings as it was in my own living of the journey that this role could not be taken on lightly or too soon.

I knew after undergrad that I wanted to help people who walked the lonely path of trauma and PTSD. I applied to New York University's Masters in Clinical Social Work program, certain that I would never get in. My early collegial efforts were beyond poor, ruffled by the inattention of a person on PTSD autopilot.

I applied anyway, thinking:

They will never let me in, but I can never say I didn't at least aspire to the highest stratosphere of my dreams.

Then I got in. It was one of the great surprises of my life.

I wanted to work with sexual trauma survivors and—having not yet read Henri Nouwen's book—I didn't think twice about it. If I had I would have realized I was nowhere near ready to go into the psychic pain of someone whose wounds were so closely aligned with my own.

It was a great blessing, disguised at the time as a great disappointment, to get my placements in graduate school in trauma, but working with every kind of trauma *but* my own.

It gave me a foundation of trauma-informed practice and time to learn healthy boundaries, build the sustainability of my own emotions, and find ways to stave off burnout.

Then, the first year into my post-internship career, in a position as a trauma therapist, I had my first sexual trauma survivor client.

She was about my age with an olive complexion and dark hair, just like me. She had been sexually assaulted multiple occasions. Her first assault was by a man she knew and later by men she didn't know. She told me her entire story in the first session. It came bubbling out like she had wanted to tell it for years. I knew the feeling.

I sat in the session, still and composed. I nodded in empathy and was supportive through her pain. The session ended and I put her next visit date on the back of my business card. Then I shook her hand and she left with words of gratitude to me for hearing her story.

I hadn't even flinched a moment during the session but the second the front door closed behind her I began to shake and felt a mix of nausea and wooziness which I remembered experiencing in my Human Sexuality class in Colorado.

Just like in Colorado, I fumbled my way out of the office, landing on the cold tile of another bathroom floor, shaking and heaving, and not completely sure what had happened.

I didn't even register it as a panic attack until my heart beat slowed down and I could get in a few deep breaths—by then nearly twenty minutes had passed.

The panic attack moment reminded me that beyond healing from my wounds I would have to address my response to other people's wounds with great care, especially those with stories so close to my own.

As Henri Nouwen explains in his book, we cannot repair in others what hasn't been repaired in ourselves.

I learned to become careful about the clients I worked with in the area of sexual trauma, and address being triggered by assessing what was best for the client *and* best for me. I began to understand that if I played the emotional martyr I would just burn out fast and then my whole pilgrimage would serve no one.

There is a unique resonance among those who have experienced trauma and battled the internal war of PTSD.

For reasons of healthy boundaries I don't disclose my trauma or PTSD history in the therapy room. I also don't hide it, so if someone comes in with foreknowledge of my history I am candid about it, but try to keep the focus on their experience. I have found that it serves no purpose to articulate it in a session. When my clients come in, it is not about me, it's about them. However, because I have sat inside that lonely dark place, I do feel I can articulate it for others in a way that makes sense.

I can be a translator between the worlds of clinical-speak and the living-experience of trauma and its aftermath.

I know what happens viscerally, but also intellectually, and I have the unique vantage point of having found my own roadmap out of PTSD. I carry the research of my own petri dish existence and healing into my clients' healing process, in whatever way it is useful for their personal journeys.

My own healing has greatly informed my practice and the therapeutic methods I use in the clinical setting.

I was healed mind, body, and spirit, inside of traditional talk therapy and in a variety of other "nontraditional" and "integrative" realms of mental health practice.

It seemed absurd to have learned so much about the nature of healing in my own recovery and not take that and give it away.

For those whose fingerprints of recovery do not mirror or resonate with my alternate healing modalities, I always try to use everything else in the toolkit until we found one that fits them.

While all trauma has inherent similarities—which creates that intuitive sense of symbiosis when meeting another trauma survivor—recovery can take so many shapes.

Yet, I continue to carry people on their journey in the best way that suits them. I use the information I have garnered on my own healing path in whatever way it helps others in their understanding and treatment of *their* darkness.

What I learned in becoming a "wounded healer" was that it was okay to set limits, find boundaries, and, yes, even end up on a bathroom floor as needed—infrequent as it may be. For me, that singular incident was the only time on record when a client's experience had such a visceral affect a personal level. It was a true teaching moment.

Not everyone is meant to be a "wounded healer," nor is anyone mandated to be, but, when we are called in that direction Nouwen says that we heal others, "in the manner in which we are wounded," and there can be great beauty and grace in that experience.

For me, it has been an abundance of grace received to do the work to help others heal in the manner in which I was wounded.

It is to be hoped that I continue to do so with humility and caution.

Let Go, Let God, and Let Love In.

I love the 12-steps and I have come to love them more intimately the more I study them. There is no principle in that process that cannot be applied to any situation of falling down, getting up, and finding transformation.

As my beloved theologian Richard Rohr says: we never find authentic transformation *without* falling down, in some way. I believe that to be true.

In falling down, the 12-steps says: let go and let God.

These are simple words with a highly complex meaning. The meaning is one that can take, and maybe should take, a lifetime to perfect.

Let go and let God.

I had finished my masters degree and begun my full time profession as a trauma therapist and was feeling pretty good.

I was competent and growing in confidence in my academic and theoretical understanding of trauma. Through my clients I was building greater awareness of the nuances of my own story and the resonance I found with each of their stories. I was realizing that my blueprint of trauma was not uniquely mine, or unique to my trauma. Intellectually I may have known that from my education and coursework on PTSD at NYU but it was fascinating to find it anecdotally replicated across the boundaries of age and across the span of all trauma, PTSD, and paths to recovery.

I also began to discover many people who had found recovery in some areas of life while being fragmented in others. Many of the survivors I met had great jobs, and equalled me in manic proficiency. Many of them had struggled with survivor guilt or shame, and some still did. The one place it seemed universally difficult to progress, for almost all of them, was making room for love—authentic, all-encompassing, self-sacrificing love.

It was my greatest area of weakness as well, even though I didn't want to see it.

To love completely you had to trust completely, let go completely, and release complete control for the sake of the other.

It was the most critical thing to a life fully lived and the one thing many of us in recovery weren't sure we could give in to. Whether it was love of a child or a spouse or a lifelong friend the all-encompassing, self-sacrificing love was a rare thing in us PTSD folk (and post-PTSD folk).

I found with them, as with myself, that it was a fear of injury, a fear of intimacy, an inability to completely trust in another that got in the way. Additionally, we were all petrified of being seen up-close, where someone might see the cracks remaining or the scars we hid.

I also realized the longer I kept love at bay the less complete everything else felt.

I was doing well at work, growing in confidence in my post-PTSD experience, and even beginning to repair my relationship with God, but I realized without letting go and letting love in, I wasn't really risking anything.

Then I met Chris. He was a divine challenge sent to me to test how badly I wanted to embrace my recovery and spiritual journey. We were sent into each other's lives to teach both of us what love really looked like. Was this romantic model of love the only path to self-sacrificing love? No, definitely not. It *was* the one I was given and, especially given the nature of my particular traumas—the traumas of rape—it was the one I had to overcome to find authentic love that could open me to the complete imperative loves: love of self, of others, of God.

Chris was in recovery (from addiction) and I was in recovery (from trauma) when we met. We both had been on our independent journeys for a number of years, and we had each mastered the individual components of healing. We had both run our lives at a manic pace to complete the necessary catch-up game—school, career, financial independence, and some manner of spiritual journey.

Although, when we met, I think neither of us had really given *all* of ourselves to anyone, yet.

We both loved books and the practice of therapy. We were both wounded healers—me with trauma survivors and he with addicts. We were both infatuated with our individual faith journeys.

Our first date was spent in Barnes and Nobles, pouring over books on philosophy and theology and talking about Frederick Nietzsche, Dietrich Bonhoeffer, CS Lewis, Richard Rohr, and Brian McLaren, among many others. We talked and drank coffee until the bookstore closed.

We were both stubborn and afraid of the change that could be imposed by letting someone else into our controlled environments of life. We were equally stubborn, strong-willed, and passionate—in all the best and worst ways—and uncertain whether we wanted to open the door, completely, to our personal universes. Our healing had gotten us that far and I think both of us were afraid of messing with a good thing. Giving in on anything, making any compromise for someone else felt scary. There was always a possibility of tripping up and falling down.

We both knew the collateral damage of falling.

Even with all those internal obstacles we fell hard for each other. Our relationship was a mix of intense intellectual sparring and mutually enveloping passion for one another. There was always that lingering feeling in the back of both our minds that felt a little like fear. It felt like standing on the edge of a cliff in a strong wind with no idea whether there were calm seas or jagged rocks below.

Our religious views, faith cultures, and spiritual origins were massively opposite and although I had thought I released my dogmatic demons, being immersed in his community touched all my hot buttons—and for him, it was the same.

Beneath the dogmas and the surface of things we were both just afraid of being with someone that could change the landscape of our lives. We were both petrified of anyone who might make us give in and give up any part of who we had become. We had each fought massive internal battles to reclaim our own selfhood.

When we met I was still very impatient and intolerant of religious places and spaces where I saw even specks of intolerance. God was testing my ability to stretch for love but I didn't understand the lesson in placing us together—both so disparate and, also, so much the same.

I still hadn't really given up the ghost and embraced the understanding that everywhere there were humans there would be fallibility—including and especially in the deepest parts of *my* selfhood.

In this realm I was still my own oxymoron because of my intolerance of intolerance, and my unwillingness to understand that intolerance existed in every community—both spiritual and secular, Protestant and Catholic, Kadampa and Tibetan Buddhist, and everywhere in between.

It was our similarity, our mutual passion for faith and God, that nearly tore us apart. He wouldn't give in on anything. I wouldn't give in on anything.

He had heard all manner of clichés about Catholics: how they were religiously lazy and worshipped idols. I never knew these stigmas and myths existed in some Christian cultures. I didn't know that in some places, and among some people, "Catholic" was a dirty word. He talked about "coins in the coffers" and "transubstantiation" like these supposedly Catholic models of religion were deal-breakers. I didn't understand where these myths had come from or how they related to the faith of my devout Catholic mother and grandmother, whose lives had greatly affected and informed my experience and understanding of God.

On my end of things, I was freaked out by the head coverings in his church, some of the fundamentalist views in the "old-guard," including words, liberally sprinkled, that always made me queasy like "believer" and "saved."

Those were words that I felt were divisive and demeaning to others. The people I had met from my past who used those words were always using them pejoratively to diminish those that didn't fit in their pie chart of Godlike human. In addition, the *actual* feminist in me—and the still-scared reflexive feminist in me—was fearful of the very limited voice for women in the public religious sphere of his community's tradition.

Catholicism was my "faith of origin" and the place I still felt closest to at-home with God at the time. It was the thread of ritual and practice through which I found my closest conduit to internal silence. Catholicism had gifted me Richard Rohr and Thomas Keating. It had been the roots of my soul and my personal origin story—named by nuns after Teresa of Avila. It was the genesis of all the Christian mystics and my sacred practice of contemplative prayer.

It was absurd, I thought, even at the time, that something I thought I would never ascribe to again— religion—was the very thing that was destroying a relationship which otherwise was full of divinity.

I couldn't see past my walls, which blocked out his dogma, to see the rigidity of my own. I couldn't see that what we were fighting about was really a space of mutuality, and neither could he.

Through feeding the monster of our mutual fears of change, love, and rigidity in the other, we broke up.

We agreed to disagree, folded our arms and called it a tie—negotiations were over. It just couldn't work.

Did we disagree about some foundational issues? Yes, but the root of what drove us apart was the fear of wanting and craving the love of the other so much it felt all-encompassing, almost addictive. We were not ready to let go, let God, and let in a love which could be all-consuming.

There was too much at stake. Everything we had built our independent empires of self on were at risk of crumbling.

Every day, all day, during our breakup, we emailed and texted. In each correspondence we fought and argued and continued to love each other even though, through our stubbornness, we refused to admit we loved each other.

It had been about a month and the 4th of July came around. I had planned a trip to the tip of Long Island, to a very tiny island called, of all things, Shelter Island.

We decided to take the trip together and see what might happen. As much as we felt we couldn't be together, there was something magnetic we couldn't let go of completely.

We drove out to the island together in his car and he stayed for the night, leaving noon-ish the following day because his grandparents were visiting from Florida. I had planned to stay another day and then take the train home to Hoboken the next morning.

We had a cautiously good time, but I think we were both at a distance, not sure if we could progress beyond this point. Shelter Island was our Switzerland, but back home we still weren't sure if we were at war.

Chris left and in the space of this tiny island with its winding dirt roads with nothing but silence and time, I began to feel spiritually overwhelmed and consumed by emotion. Something uncontrollable was flooding into me and it felt like an emotional Tsunami.

My need for control was still trying to hold on to all the reasons why I couldn't let go completely and why I couldn't give in to love. I kept thinking about the unknowables and what letting go and giving in could mean for my life and my future. I was still afraid of risking everything I had worked for—my whole recovery—for something that was uncertain, unfamiliar, and hot as iron sitting in the fire too long. My soul felt like it was burning a scalding white flame and it hurt to the point I could barely breathe.

I had been walking around the island as the feeling grew and finally, feeling like I was waiving the white flag at God, I stopped. I stopped pacing around the dirt streets in circles. I stopped reading my Rohr book searching for answers and I went to the one place I knew I didn't need to be in control and where I had to let go—contemplative prayer.

I sat on a small wood bench at the edge of a large baseball field with no other humans in sight. I took a deep breath and I closed my eyes. I asked God to free me from my own control and give me the answer of what to do about this frightening feeling that I still didn't want to call love.

Deep inhale in, deep exhale out.

Repeating the words to myself that I would come to say to many people in the years to follow, teaching contemplative prayer and practice to others: let go, let go, let go.

Let go, let go, let go. Deep inhale in, deep exhale out.

Releasing all thoughts outside of that moment I just began to call out, in my mind, a single word continuously repeating: God, God, God, God, God.

It was the only word I knew that would keep me in that moment and stop me from being locked in fear.

Then, in an instant, faster than a blink, everything that had come before and everything that could be came flooding into me—acceptance of the pain, of the missteps, of the brokenness, and on the other side of all of that only love. I felt the love of God for me, the love of me for God, and the sense that everything would be all right.

My body felt warm, but also chilled, as if every cell and molecule of me was burning with the cool heat of divine light. I was heavy and I was floating, and the brightness of light just embraced every part of me: the wounds, the scars, the beauty and the grace, all contained in me and all at peace with each other.

No more wars.

For a millisecond that felt like eternity I was able to touch beyond my own limited layer of reality and experience, viscerally, everything that was so much more.

The second I realized and identified that the moment existed, it was gone—intercepted between here and eternity with my thought of its existence. I opened my eyes, brimming with love, and I realized, for the first time, that I had been crying.

Before the feeling of certainty dissolved, like mist in the air, I picked up my phone and dialed Chris's number. I had no idea what came after this place of certainty that had come, not from me, but from God, and maybe the God *in* me, all revealed in that glimpse of everything that was and is and will be. I didn't know what came next except the impulse to call him, and to let go.

In that moment I didn't have fear or judgment or a need for control. I just had an overwhelming need to share with this one person what had just been shared with me: unconditional, unquestioning love, without an expectation of love in return or a need for reciprocation. In that moment I had a glimpse at love that never ended and didn't need validation to exist. It just was, and is, and ever shall be, world without end.

In that moment I just "was." I let go, and let God, and in return, he gifted me with love that wasn't meant to be stored up like a squirrel preparing for winter. It wasn't love to hoard, like I had hoarded all the other things I had attained since my recovery started, as if there was a shortage.

I realized something in that moment of shared grace that I would have to recall over and over for years as a reminder of what was possible in us, in the divine, and in the divine in us: never-ending and unconditional love that trumped any safety or possessions or individualistic all-American ethos.

The phone rang as I walked along the empty ballpark perimeter and then I heard him say, "Hello?"

"I don't want or need you to say anything to this. I just have to tell you something and I have no expectation of you reciprocating. I don't want you to just reflexively respond to be nice. I have to tell you one thing and you think about it and do whatever you want with it, it's yours. I love you."

Three days later, back in New Jersey, Chris asked me to come over and as we sat in the living room of his Kearny apartment, he told me he loved me too. He explained his walls and fears and worry over change and how that might impair his recovery. He told me he was afraid to lose control and feel how much he felt for me and I explained the same.

So, we stood at the cliff's edge together, wind whistling in our ears, still not sure if there were calm seas or jagged rocks below, but agreeing to face them together.

That was July. In August he proposed and on that New Year's Eve, 2008, we were married in that same Kearny living room, with a small circle of family, friends, and love around us. We were drenched in the glow of a hundred tea light candles, and in the sacred knowing that comes only out of letting go.

When we let go we are given the awareness that at every cliff's edge, if we choose to see it, there is a tether of faith and grace and divine light, holding on to us and keeping us safe.

All we have to do is let go, let God, and let love in.

Four years later, after a number of massive life changes and bumps in our intertwined lives—changing jobs, moving to Florida, buying a house, getting three dogs, dealing with illness and infertility, the reminders of the cost of bravado when we buck up against our egos, and the many pains and aches (physical, emotional, spiritual)—I still believe that is true.

I may forget it sometimes—often even—but when I come back to it, it is always true.

The divine pool of love is never-ending. We are *never* abandoned by grace, even if we stray away or forget it exists—it is always one breath, one prayer, one moment of unabashed selflessness away.

It reminds me of something a wonderful spiritual woman, and survivor in her own recovery, Rabbi Jenny asks every time she enters into faith space to lead worship with anyone, "Are you ready, are you ready, are you ready?"

To which the reply is, "I am ready, I am ready, I am ready."

All we have to do is be ready, and every moment is an opportunity for transformation and grace, and a chance to find our way out of fear and pain and sorrow.

Every moment is an opportunity. All we need is the will to let go of will, and whisper into the cosmos:

I am ready, I am ready, I am ready.

Epilogue | There is No Perfect

One of my favorite things said about trauma, PTSD, and recovery was by a licensed clinical social worker giving a presentation on the neurobiology of trauma a few years ago. Eternally a nerd at heart, neurobiology is something I have always been fascinated by because in learning how things are done in the brain, we are given the secrets to their undoing.

She said, "Just because someone is triggered it does *not* mean they have PTSD."

The reason this statement has so much value is because of the pervasive misconception I have seen in the medical, psychiatric, and PTSD survivor communities where there exists distorted belief that life will never bother you again or trigger you if you are "healed" and therefore, by those stringent guidelines no one is ever "healed" from PTSD.

By these standards I don't think any of us (in or out of trauma) could ever consider ourselves well or healed.

I think one of the most important things to understand about healing is that being rid of the diagnosis—and requisite diagnostic criteria to be met—of PTSD does not mean we will never be triggered again.

It does not mean that if we were triggered again that we are not, in fact, healed.

When I speak to my clients about this concept I tell them, "It is *not* about never being triggered again, it is about how you are able to respond when you are triggered that makes the difference between living in PTSD and living in recovery from PTSD."

❀ There is No Perfect

In life, in trauma, in pain, and in recovery there is no perfect. If we are looking for perfect in healing then we'll never find it. In each life a little imperfection must fall. That is the nature of our human experience.

Coming out of trauma, awakening and finding rebirth in life after PTSD, we have to understand there is *no* perfect. I am going to keep repeating this statement of truth because I think it needs to be repeated, and I think we are required to repeat it to ourselves like a mantra when we have doubt in our own process of healing and recovery.

There is no perfect. There is no perfect. There is no perfect.

The terms "recovery" or "healed" can be useful to contextualize the difference between active PTSD life and life after PTSD, but these words can also be intimidating or self-limiting when we become perfectionists about our own recovery.

I struggled for a long time with carrying the labels "healed" and "in recovery." I felt unsure whether I had any right to hold those titles.

Even after I began to try them on, I still questioned myself. Is this really recovery? What about that feeling I get when I walk through a parking lot at night or the occasional flinch when someone touches my shoulder from behind?

That was what was so liberating about the words I heard from the clinical social worker a number of years ago. She freed me of that last bit of uncertainty about where PTSD ends and where what I call "recovery" is allowed to begin.

So, although it doesn't fully depict the scope and nuances of life after trauma and PTSD, I carry the term "recovery" with me, insofar as it is useful to other people to see me and think, "well I can get there."

Healing takes time. Recovery is a process. And in any life *there is no perfect.*

If you remember nothing else from what I've said in the pages of this book, please carry that with you—in your pocket—and bring it out when you need a reminder. Use those words when you are beating yourself up for a backslide or a trigger response or an anxious night or a bad dream.

You are on your way. You are working hard enough.

And *there is no perfect*.

That is the nature of the process of recovery and the nature of life. We are *all* full of grace. We all have limitless potential, and we all carry the scars of *something* with us into our daily lives.

There is no perfect.

But in the imperfection we can find limitless beauty, enduring love, and endless possibility.

Acknowledgements + Thanks

Thank you to my dear friend, colleague, and fellow trauma survivor in recovery from PTSD, Michele Rosenthal, who has always pushed me to be and give more of myself and my healing experience into the world--and who was both inspiration and motivation to take this small book from my mind onto these pages.

Thank you to the many spiritual guides along my journey--both ancient and contemporary, personal and textual: Teresa of Avila, John of the Cross, Thich Nhat Hanh, Mirabai Starr, Fr. Richard Rohr, Fr. Thomas Keating, and Fr. James Martin, SJ, Tessa Bielecki, and all my beloved ladies of the Cenacle especially Mary, Sr. Barbara, and Sr. Peg. Thank you to my grandmother, Margaret Tremmel, who lives in the liminal space of my life--always my guardian and personal patron saint. Thank you to my Grandfather who is *still* always there when I need him, as he was in life.

Also, a special thanks to the many people whose living presence--momentary and otherwise--has lit the path of my sacred journey and brought me grace when I needed it most including: Mama in Laos, Mama in Pearlington, my Buddhist teacher, many of the Episcopal clergy who have been supports in my life and faith discernment, including, Chip Stokes, Kathleen Gannon, Wendy Tobias, and the ever-impressive Becca Stevens and the ladies of Thistle Farms in Tennessee. A thanks to my yoga teacher training in the Sivananda tradition and all the wonderful loving yogis I have met along the way especially those who have dedicated their life and passion for yoga to help underprivileged and emotionally wounded populations.

A thank you to the many horses I have met in my work in tandem with them on my path to be a "wounded healer." They are profound creatures who taught me so much about trust and boundaries. Thanks to the horse professionals who taught me so much about horses as healers--Maurette Hanson, Shelley Rosenberg, and Nancy Coyne, Ann Kern-Godal, Leif Hallberg, and the whole team of EFP and EFL practitioners I had the pleasure of serving with on our little brainchild professional task force.

Thank you to all my family, my husband and my three fur babies (Guinness, Gracie, and Gaia).

Thank you to all the "voices out of darkness" who helped me create the event of the same name, which inspired the completing of this book; and all the voices that were shared with me in their pain and their beauty to make "The Voices" documentary, which also influenced finally getting off my butt and finishing this book project which has been dangling in limbo for years. Thank you to some of the bravest voices out of darkness I have heard, told with such poetry and beauty: Kandy, Steph, Mike, Michele, and Kim. I carry their bravery and the power of their voice with me onto every page of this book.

A deep and soulful thank you to the music and the strength of Ani Difranco and Tori Amos, who helped me rage, weep, and smile in equal measure, in the midst of long dark nights.

Thank you to all my co-professionals and friends on the front lines of the battle against trauma and emotional wounds, especially my good friends and sisters in the fight, Marisol and Jennifer, Angela and Elaine, Dave and Jenn Nelson, and so many others who work tirelessly every day to help people heal from trauma and **all** emotional wounds.

A final thank you to the strength of *all* those who battle internal wounds and search for healing; the journey may be long and exhausting, but there is light out of darkness to be found.

Bibliography + Resources

Quote Citation:

Nouwen, Henri, *The Wounded Healer*

Referenced Persons + Texts:

Carroll, Lewis. *Alice's Adventures in Wonderland*
Avila, Teresa (of). *Interior Castle*
Frankel, Victor, *A Man's Search for Meaning.*
Keating, Thomas, *Open Mind, Open Heart: The Contemplative Dimension of the Gospel*
Nouwen, Henri, *The Wounded Healer*
Rohr, Richard, *Breathing Under Water: Spirituality and the 12 Steps*

Further Reading + Resources:

❀ Mind ❀

Doidge, Norman. *The Brain That Changes Itself: Stories of Personal Triumph from the Frontiers of Brain Science*

Figley, Charles. *An Encyclopedia of Trauma*

Herman, Judith, *Trauma and Recovery: The Aftermath of Violence*

Levine, Peter. *Waking the Tiger: Healing Trauma: The Innate Capacity to transform Overwhelming Experiences*

Naparstek, Belleruth. *Healing Journeys:Audio Series*

Pipher, Mary. *Writing To Change the World*

Redfield Jamison. *Exhuberance: The Passion for Life*

Siegel, Daniel. *Mindsight: The New Science of Personal Transformation*

Terr, Lenore. *Unchained Memories: True Stories of Traumatic Memories Lost and Found*

Tick, Edward. *War and the Soul*

Van Der Kolk, Bessel, McFarlane, Alexander, and Weisaeth, Lars. *Traumatic Stress: The Effects of Overwhelming Experinece on Mind, Body, and Society*

Williams, Mary Beth. *The PTSD Workbook: Simple, Effective Techniques for Overcoming Traumatic Stress Symptoms*

Yalom, Irvin. *Staring at the Sun: Overcoming the Terror of Death*

Zinn, Jon Kabat. *Wherever You Go, There You Are*

❈ Body ❈

Emerson, David and Hopper, Elizabeth. *Overcoming Trauma through Yoga*

Rothschild, Babette. *The Body Remembers: The psychophysiology of Trauma and Trauma Treatment*

Brown, Richard, Gerbarg, Patricia, and Muskin

Levine, Peter and Mate, Gabor. *In an Unspoken Voice: How the Body Releases Trauma and Restores Goodness*

Liebler, Nancy and Moss, Sarah. *Healing Depression the Mind-Body Way: Creating Happiness with Yoga, Meditation and Ayurveda*

Ogden, Pat, Minton, Kekuni, Pain, Clare, and Siegel, Daniel. *Trauma and the Body: A Sensorimotor Approach to Psychotherapy*

Phillip. *How to Use Herbs, Nutrients, and Yoga in Mental Health Care*

Sanford, Matthew. *Waking: A Memoir of Trauma and Transcendence*

Weintraub, Amy. *Yoga for Depression: A Compassionate Guide to Relieve Suffering through Yoga*

✸ Spirit ✸

Avila, Teresa of. *The Book of My Life*

Barks, Coleman. *Rumi:The Book of Love*

Bourgeault, Cynthia. *The Wisdom Way of Knowing: Reclaiming an Ancient Tradition to Awaken the Heart*

Chodron, Pema. *Living Beautifully: with Uncertainty and Change*

Cross, John of the. *Dark Night of the Soul*

Finley, James. *The Contemplative Heart*

Henry, Gray and Marriott, Susannah. *Beads of Faith: Pathways to Meditation and Spirituality*

Houston, Jean. *Journeys in Mythology and Sacred Psychology*

Keating, Thomas. *Divine Therapy and Addiction: Centering Prayer and the 12-Steps*

Lamott, Anne. *Traveling Mercies: Some Thoughts on Faith*

Merton, Thomas. *The Seven Storey Mountain*

Norwich, Julian of. *Showings*

Nouwen, Henri. *The Wounded Healer*

Rohr, Richard. *The Naked Now: Learning to See as the Mystics See*

Starr, Mirabai. *God of Love: A Guide to the Heart of Judaism, Christianity, and Islam*

Stewart, David. *Healing Oils of the Bible*

Teasdale, Wayne. *Discovering a Universal Spirituality in the World's Religions*

Vaughan-Lee, Llewellyn. *The Sufi's Mystical Journey Home*

Wiesel, Elie. *Open Heart*

❀ DSM Criteria for PTSD ❀

Diagnostic criteria for PTSD include a history of exposure to a traumatic event meeting two criteria and symptoms from each of three symptom clusters: intrusive recollections, avoidant/numbing symptoms, and hyper-arousal symptoms. A fifth criterion concerns duration of symptoms and a sixth assesses functioning.

Criterion A: stressor
The person has been exposed to a traumatic event in which both of the following have been present:

- The person has experienced, witnessed, or been confronted with an event or events that involve actual or threatened death or serious injury, or a threat to the physical integrity of oneself or others.
- The person's response involved intense fear, helplessness, or horror. Note: in children, it may be expressed instead by disorganized or agitated behavior.

Criterion B: intrusive recollection
The traumatic event is persistently re-experienced in at least one of the following ways:

- Recurrent and intrusive distressing recollections of the event, including images, thoughts, or perceptions. Note: in young children, repetitive play may occur in which themes or aspects of the trauma are expressed.

- Recurrent distressing dreams of the event. Note: in children, there may be frightening dreams without recognizable content
- Acting or feeling as if the traumatic event were recurring (includes a sense of reliving the experience, illusions, hallucinations, and dissociative flashback episodes, including those that occur upon awakening or when intoxicated). Note: in children, trauma-specific reenactment may occur.
- Intense psychological distress at exposure to internal or external cues that symbolize or resemble an aspect of the traumatic event.
- Physiologic reactivity upon exposure to internal or external cues that symbolize or resemble an aspect of the traumatic event

Criterion C: avoidant/numbing
Persistent avoidance of stimuli associated with the trauma and numbing of general responsiveness (not present before the trauma), as indicated by at least three of the following:

- Efforts to avoid thoughts, feelings, or conversations associated with the trauma
- Efforts to avoid activities, places, or people that arouse recollections of the trauma
- Inability to recall an important aspect of the trauma
- Markedly diminished interest or participation in significant activities
- Feeling of detachment or estrangement from others

- Restricted range of affect (e.g., unable to have loving feelings)
- Sense of foreshortened future (e.g., does not expect to have a career, marriage, children, or a normal life span)

Criterion D: hyper-arousal
Persistent symptoms of increasing arousal (not present before the trauma), indicated by at least two of the following:

- Difficulty falling or staying asleep
- Irritability or outbursts of anger
- Difficulty concentrating
- Hyper-vigilance
- Exaggerated startle response

Criterion E: duration
Duration of the disturbance (symptoms in B, C, and D) is more than one month.

Criterion F: functional significance
The disturbance causes clinically significant distress or impairment in social, occupational, or other important areas of functioning.

Acute: if duration of symptoms is less than three months
Chronic: if duration of symptoms is three months or more

References:

National Center for PTSD (www.ptsd.va.gov)
American Psychiatric Association. (2000). Diagnostic
and statistical manual of mental disorders (Revised
4th ed.). Washington, DC: Author.

❂ a healing prayer ❂

Dearest God, you hold the secrets of our hearts, the aches of our wounds, and the brokenness of our past. You carry us through hardship, and bring us to birth each and every time we need new beginnings.

You breathe with us and into us in the pain of awakenings, and let us rage into the dark nights--even and especially when we rage against you.

Wash over us with your love, invigorate our souls, and give us strength to rise, again.

Let us be inspired by your Spirit, which comforts us and reminds us it is always present, in both life's peaceful breezes and ravenous flames.

Grace us with the ability to love ourselves completely, to love you completely, and make us capable of carrying that love into the world.

We ask this as one human body, interconnected throughout time, in every culture and race and creed, woven together with the thread of hope.

Give us the capacity to have faith in ourselves, in others, and in the world as a whole, which has the potential to be mended and made whole again, and always on the precipice of regeneration.

We ask this with you, in you, and by you, as the ONE God of All ...
Now and Forever.

teresa b pasquale is a trauma therapist, yoga teacher, "crooked mystic," and 18-30's spirituality program leader within the Episcopal tradition. She is also a trauma survivor and suffered with Post Traumatic Stress Disorder (PTSD) for over 4 years before finding healing in a variety of places, faces, and graces. Now in trauma recovery she is a passionate advocate for building understanding, de-stigmatizing trauma/PTSD, and informing people that there is a way out of the broken places.

www.crookedmystic.org
www.teresabpasquale.org
www.voicesoutofdarkness.com
www.seekersdelray.org

Forthcoming Title ...

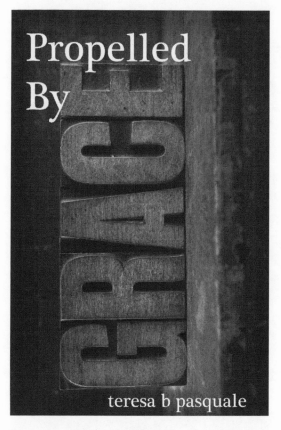

Propelled By

GRACE

teresa b pasquale

Propelled By Grace: Essays On
The Movement of God In the
World

Also Forthcoming ...

IF YOU WOULD LIKE TO SEND A
SUBMISSION EMAIL TERESA at
tbpasquale@gmail.com

For more information on VOICES OUT
OF DARKNESS you can visit:

www.voicesoutofdarkness.com

Also Forthcoming ...

Why We Need More
"MICRO-

CHURCH"

A Collection of Essays + Interviews
by Micro-Churchers Searching for
Intimacy, Community, & Sacredness in an
Impersonal World

IF YOU WOULD LIKE TO SEND A
SUBMISSION EMAIL TERESA at
tbpasquale@gmail.com

Made in the USA
Charleston, SC
06 August 2013